E-MAIL
ETIQUETTE

A FRESH LOOK AT DEALING EFFECTIVELY
WITH E-MAIL, DEVELOPING GREAT STYLE,
AND WRITING CLEAR, CONCISE MESSAGES

ST Training Solutions
Success Skills Series

SHIRLEY TAYLOR

E-MAIL
ETIQUETTE

A FRESH LOOK AT DEALING EFFECTIVELY
WITH E-MAIL, DEVELOPING GREAT STYLE,
AND WRITING CLEAR, CONCISE MESSAGES

Marshall Cavendish
Business

© 2009 Marshall Cavendish International (Asia) Private Limited
© text Shirley Taylor
© series title Shirley Taylor
Illustrations by Edwin Ng
Cover art by Opal Works Co. Limited

Published by Marshall Cavendish Business
An imprint of Marshall Cavendish International
1 New Industrial Road, Singapore 536196

Other Marshall Cavendish Offices
Marshall Cavendish Ltd. 5th Floor 32–38 Saffron Hill, London EC1N 8FH · Marshall Cavendish Corporation. 99 White Plains Road, Tarrytown NY 10591-9001, USA · Marshall Cavendish International (Thailand) Co Ltd. 253 Asoke, 12th Flr, Sukhumvit 21 Road, Klongtoey Nua, Wattana, Bangkok 10110, Thailand · Marshall Cavendish (Malaysia) Sdn Bhd, Times Subang, Lot 46, Subang Hi-Tech Industrial Park, Batu Tiga, 40000 Shah Alam, Selangor Darul Ehsan, Malaysia

Marshall Cavendish is a trademark of Times Publishing Limited

National Library Board Singapore Cataloguing in Publication Data

Taylor, Shirley.
    E-mail etiquette : a fresh look at dealing effectively with e-mail, developing great style, and writing clear, concise messages / by Shirley Taylor. – Singapore : Marshall Cavendish Business,– c2009.
    p. cm. – (Success skills series)
    Includes index.
    ISBN-13 : 978-981-261-673-9
    ISBN-10 : 981-261-673-X

    1. Electronic mail messages. 2. Commercial correspondence.
    3. Online etiquette. I. Title. II. Series: Success skills series (ST Training Solutions)

HD30.37
651.79 — dc22   OCN313955248

Printed in Singapore by Times Printers Pte Ltd

PREFACE

Congratulations on picking up this copy of *E-mail Etiquette*. I'm very proud that this is one of the first books in the ST Training Solutions 'Success Skills' series. This series includes several short, practical books on a range of topics that will help you develop your skills and enhance your success at work and in your personal life too.

The 'Success Skills' series was originally created to meet the needs of participants of ST Training Solutions public workshops. After attending one of our workshops, many participants expressed a real desire to continue learning, to find out more about the topic, to take it to another level. They were hungry for knowledge. Just the effect I hoped for when I set up ST Training Solutions Pte Ltd in 2007. With the 'Success Skills' series of books, the experience and expertise of our trainers can be enjoyed by many more people.

As Series Editor, I've enjoyed working with authors to make sure the books are easy-to-read, highly practical, and written in straightforward, simple language. Every book is packed with essential tools and strategies that will make you more effective and successful. We've included illustrations that reinforce some key points, because I believe we learn more if we add some fun and humour. You'll also notice some key features that highlight important learning points:

Myth Buster

Here you will find a statement that is not true, with notes on the true facts of the matter.

Fast Fact

Useful snippets of information or special points to remember.

Aha! Moment

This is a 'light bulb' moment, when we note something you may be able to conclude from a discussion. Don't forget to note your own 'Aha! Moments' perhaps when you receive some extra insight that clarifies an important point.

Try This

Here you'll find a suggestion for how you can put a special point into practice, either at home or at work.

Danger Zone

You'll find some words of warning here, such as things to avoid or precautions to take.

Star Tips

At the end of each chapter you'll find a list of Star Tips — important notes to remind you about the key points.

By picking up this book you have already shown a desire to learn more. The solid advice and practical guidelines provided in this book will show you how you can really go from good to great!

Good luck!

Shirley Taylor

Shirley Taylor
Series Editor
CEO, ST Training Solutions Pte Ltd

 **ST Training Solutions**

www.shirleytaylortraining.com
www.shirleytaylor.com

CONTENTS

INTRODUCTION

E-mail is possibly one of the greatest inventions of our lifetime. It's having a phenomenal effect on the way we communicate, but that may not always be for the better! Reading, writing and managing e-mail is taking an increasing amount of our time. However, research shows that the major cause of e-mail stress is not its volume but its inappropriate use as a communication tool.

More of us have taken to using e-mail to stay in touch while we are travelling or working from home, using not just desktops and laptops, but also handheld devices. We are using e-mail to communicate with friends and family, as well as with business contacts, both at home and overseas. Perhaps we can relax standards a little in our personal e-mails, but e-mailing for business purposes has reached a new dimension. People whose jobs never used to involve writing skills are now finding themselves replying to dozens of e-mails every day.

Most of us comment about the increasing quantity of the messages we receive and the pressure we are under to respond quickly. But when we are under such pressure, what happens to the quality of the messages we exchange?

The bottom line remains: just as a handshake and eye contact say something about you and your organisation when you meet someone in person, the approach you take in an e-mail gives an impression as well. Whether you are writing a thank you note, a meeting reminder, a proposal or a sales pitch, what you write and how you write it affects what people think of you, and it affects the image of your organisation.

A well-written message that looks and sounds professional will make it easier for people to want to do business with you. It will help people feel good about communicating with you. It will also help you achieve the right results.

The fact that you've picked up this book means that you want to make e-mail work for you, not against you. You are interested in improving your reputation as a caring communicator, as someone who uses e-mail thoughtfully. You also want to use e-mail in ways that present you and your organisation in a positive light.

I hope you'll practice the guidelines I've shared in this book, and that you'll find the techniques useful. It's a book that I hope you will keep on your bookshelf, dipping into it occasionally as you learn and experience more.

Start turning the pages and enjoy the huge rewards it will bring!

Shirley Taylor
www.shirleytaylortraining.com
www.shirleytaylor.com

ASSESS YOURSELF

What is your current understanding of e-mail?

1. Why shouldn't you type your messages in ALL CAPS?

a) ALL CAPS implies that I am shouting or yelling.

b) It causes a strain on your eyes and makes reading more difficult.

c) It makes the writer look lazy and uneducated.

d) All of the above.

2. The most important thing to do with every e-mail message is:

a) Spell check, use full sentences and proper grammar.

b) Use proper paragraphs and leave a space between paragraphs.

c) Make sure the e-mail address is correct.

d) All of the above.

3. You should only forward an e-mail when:

a) You feel it is important.

b) You know the other person should have the information.

c) You include a personal comment about why you are forwarding this message to this specific person.

d) The topic is commendable and important for other people to read.

4. When replying to e-mails you should down-edit your reply by:

a) Spell checking the sender's previous e-mail.

b) Removing previous signature files.

c) Removing the oldest two e-mails in the sequence.

d) Removing everything that's not essential to the ongoing conversation.

5. If you can't reply to a message straight away, what should you do?

a) Send a brief acknowledgement and say you'll reply as soon as possible.

b) Carry on with your other work; you'll get round to it later.

c) Put it in a special 'KIV' or 'pending' folder.

d) Delete it.

6. When is it all right to contact people by e-mail about your business?

a) When I know they really need my service.

b) Anytime at all — after all, lots of companies do 'cold calling' on the telephone.

c) Only when they call or e-mail me and ask me for information.

d) When I know I can save them money.

7. A good way to check the user-friendliness of your message is to:

a) Use lots of abbreviations so my message is short and simple.

b) Run a spell check because that finds all the errors.

c) Write it all in one paragraph so the message is not too long.

d) Read it out loud with proper tone as if I am speaking to the recipient.

8. A good subject line is:

a) Lengthy, to give as much information as possible.

b) Specific, meaningful, appropriate, relevant and thoughtful.

c) One or two words only.

d) You don't always need to use a subject line.

9. When you receive a spam e-mail message, the best thing to do is:

a) Read it just in case it's interesting.

b) Delete it.

c) Forward it to my friends.

d) Reply with an angry, abusive message telling them to stop spamming.

10. You can create good rapport with clients by:

a) Always using e-mail instead of picking up the phone.

b) Using standard phrases and corporate templates.

c) Using friendly language and a chatty style, as if having a conversation.

d) Being very serious and formal in all my e-mails.

How did you do?

1. The correct answer is (d). Capitals means much more than shouting. Learn more about what's right and what's not in Chapters 2 and 5.

2. Did you answer (d)? All these things are important. See Chapter 2 for a list of common complaints about e-mail in practice.

3. It is always good to know why you are receiving a specific e-mail, so please follow the advice in (c). If you need more help, Chapter 3 is for you.

4. (d) is the correct answer here. Find out more about good e-mail habits in Chapters 5, 6 and 7.

5. It's good manners to send a brief acknowledgement, so (a) is the correct answer here. See Chapter 3 for an example.

6. Please don't spam. The correct answer is (c). Learn more about practising safe e-mail in Chapter 9.

7. The golden rule of writing today is to write as if you are speaking, so I do hope you answered (d). Learn more about writing great messages in Chapters 5, 6 and 7.

8. A good subject line is SMART — so the answer is (b). Spruce up your writing skills by referring to Chapter 4.

9. Whatever you do, don't reply. Just hit 'Delete', so (b) is the answer. Check out more about the dreaded scourge of the Internet in Chapter 9.

10. You will create a good rapport with everyone if you use a chatty style as if you are having a conversation. Find out more about building great relationships with your readers in Chapter 8.

THE AGE OF E-MAIL

"Computers are magnificent tools for the realisation of our dreams, but no machine can replace the human spark of spirit, compassion, love, and understanding."

Sir Louise Gerstner

The Internet is rapidly developing its own unique culture formed by a diverse group of people of various religions, nationalities, genders and experiences. The Internet, commonly known as cyberspace, is a worldwide melting pot of opinions and ideas, used by people known as netizens (network citizens). Netizens are part of a social and cultural evolution in a new community of people. They are adventurers on an electronic frontier, where their individual voices can be heard, and can change and shape the future of electronic communication as we know it.

The Internet is a place where global information and communication is constantly expanding and evolving. Just as with any culture, there are customs that provide guidelines and cohesiveness to the people involved. That's what this book is all about — helping you understand the rules of the road for e-mail.

The impact of e-mail on business

E-mail is the most popular facility available through the Internet. Relatively cheap to use, messages can be sent anywhere in the world at a cost of no more than a local telephone call. One of the most profound effects of e-mail has been the way it's changed the way people work. Let's look at some of the changes that have taken place in the way businesses operate — some of which are good, and others, not so good.

- Traditionally, secretaries would open their employer's mail and could keep up-to-date on everything. Now that many managers read their own e-mail, a secretary's role could be quite frustrating unless a good understanding has been achieved with employers and some good ground rules laid down.

- Since many executives read their own mail, it is often possible to contact powerful people directly. But remember, not all CEOs are keen to receive information directly. Even if you know your CEO's e-mail address, it doesn't always mean that he wants to hear directly from just anyone. Your own line manager may also be unhappy with you for going over his or her head in such a way.

- Some people get so used to doing everything over e-mail that they ignore, forget about or don't give as much importance to paper mail. Make sure you check and deal with your snail mail at least once a day.

- Some people receive dozens of messages every day, some that are important, others that are being sent to them 'just in case', when they don't really need to see them. As a result, many people find they are spending more than half their time dealing with e-mail. We can all do our part to ease this problem by learning to respect other people's time, and only forward e-mails to the people who really need to see them.

- Some people send the same message several times because of errors they spotted the first (or second) time after they've sent an e-mail out. Correct your mistakes before you hit the 'Send' button. You will look a whole lot better to your readers if you get it right the first time.

- Very often, working with e-mail means you have to develop a good memory. We tend not to print out as many messages as we perhaps should. Also, many companies implement a system whereby old messages (say 30 days old) may be deleted automatically from your workstation so that the hard disk is not clogged up unnecessarily. Protect yourself by saving paper copies of important messages.

- Many people are sending e-mail messages instead of picking up the phone. This is a common complaint when I talk to clients to discuss potential in-house training. They really want to impress on their staff that sometimes it is best to speak to people directly. On e-mail it may take several back and forth messages to reach a satisfactory conclusion when the issue could be resolved in one phone call.

- E-mail enables people to work from home more effectively while staying in touch with the office. Many workers, particularly those with young children, value the flexibility that working from home offers.

- There has been an increase in the number of 'virtual workers'. Because it's so easy to keep in touch, people are choosing a home office, and working with staff who also prefer to work from their own home office. Regular discussion over the phone and on e-mail means everyone can be kept up-to-date on projects, and of course traditional office costs are reduced. One thing home workers need much more of, however, is self-discipline and motivation.

- Commuting time, on flights and train journeys, can be usefully spent dealing with your e-mail messages and sorting out your inbox.

As there have been no real guidelines laid down on how to work with e-mail or how to write e-mail messages, some frustrations are inevitable. A major problem for some people is simply being unable to adjust their communication styles to this new medium. When e-mail is used effectively it can be very powerful indeed. However, when it is used ineffectively it can be costly, annoying and damaging to a company's reputation.

Aha! Moment

E-mail is a 'double-edged sword'. There are many favourable and unfavourable consequences that result from the emergence of e-mail.

Fast Fact

Current statistics show that there are around 210 billion e-mails being sent every day — that means more than 2 million e-mails per second. And get this: approximately 70 per cent of them are probably spam and viruses! Genuine e-mails are sent by around 1.3 billion e-mail users.

Consequences of e-mail

Internal consequences

Traditionally, internal communication in business was hierarchical, with messages being passed up and down the chain, often with secretaries acting as a filter between managers and staff. Flatter company structures have changed the whole spectrum of internal communication. A network has now replaced the hierarchical model. With e-mail, every member of staff is able to communicate directly with everyone else — up, down and across the organisation. This flatter organisation structure, and new power of employees to communicate company-wide, has meant that information can be distributed more efficiently around the organisation. However, because of the relative ease of sending e-mail, messages may sometimes be sent without due thought and consideration.

External consequences

E-mail has undoubtedly helped us to establish and maintain business relationships with branches, clients and suppliers. Relationships with customers and co-workers can be improved and productivity can be enhanced considerably through effective use of e-mail.

An external e-mail message in particular is as much an ambassador for your organisation as a business letter. The impression you make comes from more than just the words you use too. Your readers will also be looking at the language you use, as well as the tone you use to convey your message. The way you display your message visually and the way you structure the paragraphs will also have a significant impact on your reader's ability to pick out the main points.

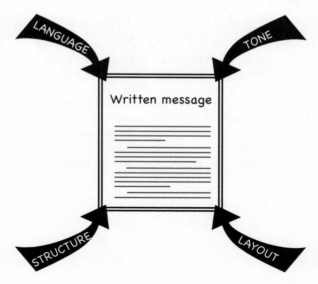

If we are to earn the trust and confidence of our readers when sending e-mails, it's important to pay attention to all these things, as well as one other key ingredient — style. Style in written communication means attention to proper spelling and punctuation, proper sentence construction instead of non-sentences, full spellings instead of abbreviations suitable only for sms. Style means being creative in what you write and how you write. It also means making your communication look visually-attractive (i.e. leaving a line space between paragraphs, using numbered points or bullets, also consistency).

Aha! Moment

If we are to achieve our objectives and get the right results from our e-mails, we need to pay real attention to much more than the words we use.

Myth Buster

We don't need training in how to use e-mail. We can pick it up with experience.

Wrong! Many organisations provide a wide range of training for employees — from supervisory training to communication skills, from leadership skills to powerful presentations. In view of the increasing impact that communication has on business, I'm glad to see that many companies are providing training in effective business writing — not only for business letters and reports, but also for e-mail.

Why do we love e-mail?

In terms of the time factor alone, it's easy to see why e-mail is the preferred choice for written communication. Let's take a look at some more reasons why we love e-mail:

- **It's written.** You can edit and check it before you send it. The recipient can read it, forward it to someone else, print it out and file it away.

- **It's time-zone friendly.** E-mail is great for international communication over different time zones.

- **It's quick.** Messages are usually delivered in seconds. (They may not be read so quickly, but they will be in the recipient's inbox.)

- **It's cheap.** Of course you need to buy a computer and a modem, and (sometimes) pay an Internet service provider. But no matter where your recipient is, each message should cost no more than a local phone call.

- **It's flexible.** You can forward or send multiple copies of messages easily, and attach documents to messages without any hassle.

- **You can attach files.** As long as your recipient has the software to open it, you can attach a spreadsheet, a report, photographs, a game, a video — virtually anything!

- **It's non-intrusive.** You decide when to read your mail and when to reply.

- **It can be prioritised.** When you open your e-mail first thing in the morning you can prioritise your e-mail-related work for the day. Simple or urgent tasks can be dealt with quickly before getting involved in more heavy-duty or non-urgent work.

- **You see the history of each communication.** This is a great tool so you can scroll down and remind yourself about previous discussions on the topic.

Danger Zone

Avoid the temptation of keeping your e-mail alert switched on the whole time. If you are working on an important report or spreadsheet, you need to focus. You can't concentrate if your pop-up keeps popping up every few minutes, or if that 'ding' keeps 'dinging'! Be sensible and switch off your e-mail alert when you need to concentrate.

Handheld electronic devices

E-mail doesn't only come to our desks. Many of us now carry e-mail around with us on our mobile phones. This often results in being on call 24 hours a day, every day, even on weekends. Apart from never being free from the demands of work, this also leads to another problem: messages typed with our thumbs often contain errors and can end up becoming quite terse. You might include a tagline such as 'Sent from my Blackberry handheld', thinking that your recipient may be more forgiving of mistakes or brusqueness. However, I'm not convinced that this will always work.

A friend recently told me that he now does 75 per cent of his e-mailing through his Blackberry and that he has to adapt his language for this new medium. Things he would not normally do on his computer, such as abbreviating words or not starting off with a greeting, he is actually doing on his electronic device.

Consider this message that he may have sent if he'd been sitting at his computer:

> *Hi John*
>
> *Great to hear from you. I'm glad you can come down to Singapore next week to discuss this exciting project. If you can let me have your proposal within the next couple of days, I can discuss it with our management and send you any urgent questions for your consideration before we meet.*
>
> *Look forward to seeing you.*
> *Michael*

If sending this same message from his electronic device, the message would become:

> *Pls send yr proposal so I can put to mgnt and send you any q's. Tnks.*

> *(Sent from my Blackberry Wireless Handheld)*

You can see what I mean about the message becoming terse, not to mention abbreviated. It could actually ruin the personal rapport that he may have built up with this recipient. Such abbreviated messages may also lead to more back and forth e-mailing for clarification, which may not be necessary if he had either picked up the phone or waited till he could give the message a more considered response.

Another concern is the tendency to become addicted to checking our handhelds constantly. Imagine you are down town on your way to an appointment and you bump into a client. While you're standing on the street side having a discussion with her, she sneaks a peak at her electronic device. How are you going to feel about that? Not impressed, right? Never underestimate the importance of body language, especially in making eye contact (and that means with the other person, not with your Blackberry!)

It's worse if you check your e-mail on your electronic device in formal meetings, or sneakily try to send a text message imagining that no one will notice. Everyone notices!

 Danger Zone

Etiquette applies to handhelds too. Avoid checking your handheld during dinner, at a cinema or concert, in a meeting, in the playground with your children, or when out on a date!

E-mail enhances efficiency

It's important to continually keep up with technology that makes it easier to stay in touch with customers and colleagues. But e-mail should not be taken for granted. This fabulous technology should be looked upon as a tool to enhance communication rather than a replacement for communication. E-mail is a wonderful tool that makes it possible for us to achieve more, with greater efficiency and professionalism. Remember though, that e-mail is only a supplement and should never replace human interaction.

Let's look at just a few other ways in which e-mail is helping us to increase our efficiency:

- **Connection to people and information.** E-mail helps you to stay informed and keeps other people informed more effectively than would be possible if we didn't have it.

- **Improved project management.** With such a global community these days, working together on a project can prove to be quite difficult when people are in different companies, places and time zones. E-mail makes this process so much easier.

- **Team building.** E-mail is helping to make group work more effective. All team members must be briefed with a common set of objectives so that they realise the importance of replying promptly to all team mail. They also need compatible software so that they can attach and read all the documents that will be sent among members.

- **Global communication.** With Internet connections, it's possible to reach out way beyond the boundaries of your organisation. You can join discussion groups and mailing lists relating to your specific interests, and subsequently engage in discussions with thousands of people around the world.

- **Better record management.** With e-mail now often replacing telephone conversations, letters and memos, much of the information is in one place, so it becomes easier to manage. All messages regarding a specific topic can be kept in a special folder. Alternatively a search will quickly call up all the messages that meet certain criteria.

- **Virtual meetings.** Before e-mail came about, many more meetings took place. It is sometimes quite difficult to get lots of people together at the same venue and time, and with pressures of work, it could be a week or more before everyone involved could get together. E-mail solves this problem. A message can be sent to everyone involved, the issue or problem can be discussed with everyone being copied, and a lot of time can be saved.

- **Collaborative work.** E-mail makes it easy and cheap to share photographs, graphics, files, even video. Whether your colleague is in the next office or at the other side of the world, distance is no longer an issue. As long as everyone has compatible versions of the necessary software, it's easy to attach anything to an e-mail message.

Aha! Moment

While it's important to keep up-to-date with new technology, this shouldn't be taken to the extent that we avoid talking to our customers and colleagues personally. E-mail is a supplement to, not a replacement for, interaction. It's a useful tool that helps us to create more time and more opportunities for everyone in the organisation to do even better.

International considerations

In my workshops I'm often asked what it means when someone begins an e-mail with, "I hope this e-mail finds you well." This seems to be a very misunderstood greeting, but it simply means, "I hope you are fine today." This emphasises the importance of using appropriate language when e-mailing people from another country, or whose mother tongue may not be English. Be cautious about overusing idiomatic phrases that everyone around you understands but may be difficult to understand by someone not absolutely fluent in your language.

In general, when e-mailing people whose mother tongue is not English, it is best to use short, simple sentences that will be much easier to understand. Keep your messages as short as possible without letting meaning suffer and use simple words instead of long ones. Niceties are acceptable, to a point, but please don't overdo it. Learn more about simplifying your language in Chapter 5.

When crossing international boundaries with your e-mails, it's better to err on the side of caution and use a more formal tone for your messages at first. It will then be easy to progress from formal to friendly as you get to know your recipient better. It would weaken your position if you have to step backwards from friendly to formal.

Interacting with groups on the Internet

The term 'netiquette' means, in essence, 'network etiquette' — social conventions that facilitate interaction over networks. This includes mailing lists, blogs, discussion groups, forums, and of course, e-mail. In this book we are mainly covering e-mail etiquette. However, it may be useful to mention various other forms of interaction here because these also involve sending messages via our keyboards.

- **Discussion groups**

  The growth of the Internet has given rise to many online discussion sites, which are also known as Internet forums or message boards. They are the modern equivalent of a traditional bulletin board. These forums consist of a group of contributors who usually must be registered with the system and who become known as 'members'. Individual members submit topics for discussion (known as 'threads') and they communicate with each other using 'posts' (publicly visible messages), or private messaging (messages sent from a member to one or more other members). People participating in an Internet forum will usually develop connections with each other, and interest groups usually form around discussion on specific topics. The term 'community' has become known as the segment of online users participating in the activities of the website they reside in. This is also used to refer to the group rather than just the site.

- ## Chat rooms

  A 'chat room' is a place where you can have an interactive conversation. You key in messages on your screen and they will be seen by all other people in the same chat room, and of course vice versa. Chat room services are provided by some organisations as a way to provide online help and to serve as a two-way exchange with customers.

- ## Blogs

  The word 'blog' is a contraction of the term 'web log'. Blogs are usually maintained by individuals who regularly enter commentary and articles. Some blogs provide information and news on a specific subject, while others serve more as online diaries. An important part of blogging is the interactive format where readers can leave comments.

In general, people who take part in discussion groups, chat rooms and blogs generally use a more casual style of writing. Abbreviations and emoticons are considered acceptable, and grammatical and spelling errors are forgiven more easily than on e-mail.

Star Tips for making the most of e-mail

1. Adapt your communication style to make e-mail work for you, not against you.

2. Use e-mail appropriately to enhance your reputation and your organisation's image.

3. Switch off your e-mail alert when you need to concentrate or focus on an important project.

4. Consider if a quick word with a colleague or a simple phone call to a client could resolve an issue more efficiently than using e-mail.

5. Enhance relationships with colleagues and clients by using e-mail effectively.

6. Pay attention to the tone, language and structure of e-mails, as all these impact your reader.

7. Don't let e-mail be a replacement for communication. It is a tool for enhancing communication.

8. When e-mailing across cultures, keep your language simple and your sentences short.

THE PITFALLS AND THE POTENTIAL OF E-MAIL

"After all, computers crash, people die, relationships fall apart. The best we can do is breathe and reboot."

Carrie Bradshaw,
from *Sex and the City*

2

Because of the apparent ease of sending an e-mail message, computer systems are being flooded with an excessive amount of information. This great avalanche of e-mail is also causing its share of problems. When e-mail is used effectively it can be very powerful indeed. But when it is used ineffectively it can be costly and annoying, and can also damage a person's, and an organisation's, reputation.

Understanding and appreciating what can go wrong with e-mail, and the many problems e-mail brings, will help you to turn the problems around and change them into useful potential for you and your company to maximise.

Seven deadly sins of working with e-mail
Read this list of seven deadly sins of working with e-mail, and tick the ones that apply to you. If you tick a few of these items, you need help. You'll find it in this chapter.
1. Your e-mail messages often bounce back because of an error in the address.
2. You sometimes wish you could backtrack after sending a message, but it's too late.
3. You are frequently interrupted throughout the day with a constant flow of e-mail messages.
4. You have sometimes sent messages via e-mail when you know a telephone call would have been better.
5. You haven't done any housekeeping or deleted any messages for a long time.
6. You sometimes send messages off quickly without a greeting or a sign-off, and without checking and proofreading carefully.
7. You have sent private or confidential messages via e-mail, which you have regretted.

What can go wrong with e-mail?

Just as snail mail can be delivered to the wrong address or get lost in the post, e-mail also has its share of quirks. Problems can occur with your computer, with your ISP or with the recipient's computer. Here are some common shouts for help:

1.   I can't get connected

The most common reason that your computer cannot connect to your ISP's service is if you're using the wrong user name or password. Check these carefully, especially your password, which may be case-sensitive (care is needed to use upper and lower case letters consistently).

If you still encounter problems, and you have checked the obvious cables, modem and phone lines, you may need to check some internal settings on your computer. If you have checked these and you are still having problems, you may need to call your ISP's telephone helpline.

2.   My e-mail has been returned

Sometimes e-mail messages cannot be delivered, so they bounce back to you. When this happens you will receive something called a 'mailer-daemon' — a failed-mail message with a heading something like 'Returned mail: user unknown'. The most likely cause is that you made a mistake in the address. Alternatively it could be due to problems with the destination computer or within the network. In that case try sending the message again later.

3.   I clicked 'Send' but I want to stop the message from being sent

If you are working offline you can simply delete the message from your outbox. If you are online when you press 'Send', then there is nothing you can do to stop it. Within seconds it will arrive at its destination.

4.   I've received a message about a virus warning

You may receive messages warning you about computer viruses being spread via e-mail. A lot of such messages are circulating. Many of them are hoaxes, so don't be taken in by these. You cannot get a virus by opening an e-mail message. But you can get one by opening an attachment, which can cause serious damage.

5.   I've received a message saying I could win big prizes

These messages are also hoaxes. Don't forward them to anyone else. In particular if the message asks you to 'click here' (to ultimately take you to a URL), on no account do so. I (rather naively) did so once, and within hours an unscrupulous e-mailer had downloaded my password and sent out a message to 2,500 people from my e-mail address book. The message contained abusive messages and pornographic filth. Fortunately my ISP was informed about this and they scrambled my password immediately, making it impossible for the same person to use my address again.

Why don't we love e-mail?

I did a survey asking people about problems they are experiencing with e-mail. Here is a summary of what I found out. Hopefully these will give you some strategies to help you manage your e-mail.

1.   Constant interruptions to your working day

Most e-mail programmes have an instant messaging facility that means you are interrupted regularly by a little bell or a voice that says 'You've got mail'. These interruptions can interfere with your planned work and add frustration and stress to your workload. In some companies, however, staff say they must leave their alert on all the time because their boss insists, in case something urgent is missed. Unless it's a specific requirement of your job, you must consider switching off your e-mail alert — you will be able to focus on your report or your spreadsheet, and you will feel a greater sense of achievement by doing so. Then you can go back to your e-mail and give it your full attention.

2.   It wastes time

Composing and replying to e-mails can sometimes take up a lot of time that could be better spent on your real job. However, it is common courtesy to reply to e-mail as soon as possible, even if it's just an acknowledgement saying you will give the matter more attention and get back to the writer later.

A participant in one of my workshops told me that he tries never to click on an e-mail message more than twice. He said, "I always try to respond as soon as I've read a message, or delete it. If I'm pushed for time, I scan all my messages and then answer the urgent ones straight away. I then deal with the others whenever I have a free moment."

3.   It's not always the best choice of medium

It can sometimes take the exchange of many e-mail messages to resolve a situation or a problem that could have been dealt with swiftly and efficiently by a telephone call or face-to-face discussion. Before you send an e-mail message, ask yourself if it really is the best way to deliver the message. It may be convenient and quick, but it would not be suitable, for example, for passing on bad news or dealing with an uncomfortable situation. In such cases, a telephone call or even a face-to-face discussion may be much better.

 Aha! Moment

Handling a delicate or sensitive situation is better done by the human voice, either in person or on the phone, as it can convey sympathy and/or other emotions.

4.   Confidentiality can be a problem

Keeping something confidential is almost impossible with e-mail. Your employer may have the right to read — without your consent or knowledge — any e-mail messages you send or receive at work. Therefore, be careful what you write — it may come back to haunt you!

5.   E-mail overload

The traffic problem seems to be one of the main issues with e-mail. Some managers receive hundreds of messages every day, so ways to deal with this overload must be developed. It's too easy to forward messages on to lots of people, whether or not they really need to see them, 'just in case'. This can cause extreme annoyance as well as overloading networks, not to mention being a complete waste of people's time.

 Fast Fact

Many organisations issue instructions to employees to keep individual mailbox size down. Once a mailbox exceeds that limit, employees are unable to send out or receive messages. This forces staff to keep their mailboxes to a manageable size, and enforces good housekeeping habits. This system works very well in most organisations and is also is cost-effective.

6.   Overflowing inboxes

E-mail messages that are not deleted are causing not a paper mountain but an electronic mountain, so you must do your filing regularly. Make some time to go through messages and delete those you no longer need. And if you receive copies of e-mail messages that you don't really need to see, tell the sender so that it doesn't happen again.

7.   Increased stress levels

It's official. Research shows that one of the top 10 causes of workplace stress is the pressure of keeping up with e-mail messages. This ranks higher than having a bad relationship with your boss and dealing with customer complaints! It's a real problem. Let experience point the way to letting e-mail work for you, instead of against you.

8.   More haste, less speed

Many people feel that because it's e-mail, it has to be acted on instantly. This is adding to the pressures that people already face. Not only this, but because e-mail is seen as urgent, some writers don't take much care with spelling, punctuation, grammar or structure. So what's happening is that rushed messages become garbled, with spelling, grammar and punctuation errors, poor structure, and with no real focus. The end result is that such messages are not effective and lead to that inevitable 'ding-dong' of further e-mails to clarify!

9.   Junk e-mail or spam

Some people are using e-mail to send unsolicited advertising, called 'junk e-mail' or 'spam'. We will look at how to deal with this in Chapter 9.

10. Death of conversation

People who used to speak to each other regularly are nowadays communicating via e-mail. Sometimes when my phone rings and it's a voice I usually communicate with on e-mail, I say "Oh hello ... a real voice! How wonderful to TALK to you!" So please, pick up the telephone now and again — it's great to talk!

Top 10 complaints about e-mail in practice

I was very grateful to many people who responded to a survey that I carried out asking them to share with me their main complaints about e-mail in practice. Here are some common complaints that I heard. If you use e-mail regularly I'm sure you will be nodding your head in agreement with some of these.

1. Vague subject line

People will sometimes not even read a message unless the subject line captures their attention in the first place. Busy people with lots of messages every day just do not have the time. Help your reader to understand the bigger picture by composing a clear subject line that tells the reader exactly what the message is all about. Your subject line should be brief (many mailers will cut off long subject lines) and should give the essence of the content of the message. See SMART subject lines in Chapter 4.

Danger Zone

A message that is sent with an empty subject line or one that says 'Help me!' or 'Urgent' will probably end up in the recipient's trash. A good subject line will not only help the recipient, it will also help you by ensuring your message is read.

2.   No greeting and no sign-off

Nothing annoys me more than receiving a message from someone that doesn't begin with a simple greeting, or end with the name of the person who sent it. Please remember the simple courtesies of a greeting and sign off. You can see more about what's acceptable in Chapter 6.

3.   Just plain sloppy

As more people use e-mail, sloppy work is becoming more of a problem. Common complaints include:

- not being clear on the goal of the e-mail
- not attempting to develop a logical flow of ideas
- not doing spell check
- poor typing habits
- treating e-mail more like a quick chat rather than as a concise written document

4.   Use the right case

Sloppy work sometimes results in writers using ALL CAPITALS or lower case abbreviations. In the world of e-mail, using capital letters is equivalent to SHOUTING! (Didn't you automatically raise your voice then, even when reading this to yourself?) This is seen as rude and annoying, and it should not be necessary even to put a subject line in capital letters. Other people (perhaps because they are trying to mask their lack of grammar skills?) cannot be bothered with any capital letters at all, and this can be very frustrating, as can abbreviations like the ones seen in the following message. Sometimes a message can be abbreviated so much that it can be very difficult to read.

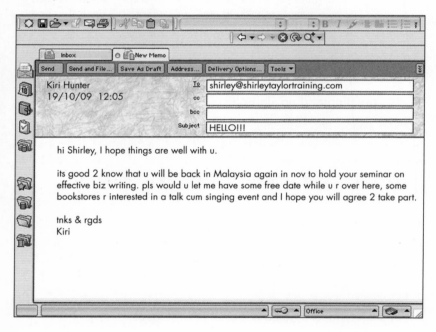

hi Shirley, I hope things are well with u.

its good 2 know that u will be back in Malaysia again in nov to hold your seminar on effective biz writing. pls would u let me have some free date while u r over here, some bookstores r interested in a talk cum singing event and I hope you will agree 2 take part.

tnks & rgds
Kiri

5. Bad grammar, spelling and punctuation

A quick way to lower your credibility is to send out messages with spelling, punctuation or grammar errors. Remember that your messages give an impression of your organisation and of you as an individual. Make sure it is a good impression by taking as much care when composing an e-mail message as you would with a formal letter. For more advice on sprucing up your cyber-grammar skills, see Chapter 8.

6. Poor formatting

Some people just ramble on and on in their messages, with no spaces or breaks between paragraphs. Talk about showing no respect for the reader's time or ease of understanding! If you write long-winded sentences with no paragraphing and no blank lines between paragraphs, your message will not be easy to read, and that will not do your reputation any good. For help in putting together an effective message, see Chapter 6.

7. Vague messages

Another common comment in my survey was from people who said they received messages in which it was difficult to figure out what action was needed. E-mail messages are often sent in such a rush that the writer does not plan the message beforehand and makes no effort to structure it properly. Other writers ramble on in long-winded epistles that miss the point altogether. Such messages rarely achieve their objectives and will only frustrate and confuse.

8. Unfriendly tone

The most difficult thing to convey in e-mail is emotions. This often gets people into trouble because they type out exactly what they would say without thinking of the tone of voice that would be used to signal their emotions. It is therefore easy for misunderstandings to occur in e-mail. When sending e-mail, remember that readers could be put on the defensive if your tone is not quite right. Learn more about touching up your tone in Chapter 5.

9.   CC the whole wide world

One common aggravation of e-mail users is that they are sent copies of e-mail messages just for the sake of it, or are forwarded copies of long messages that they don't really need to see. Think very carefully about who needs to see a copy of your e-mail message. Send messages to everyone who needs to know, not to everyone you know!

 Fast Fact

> In the days when we really did use carbon paper, CC meant 'carbon copy', and BCC 'blind carbon copy'. However, in today's technological age, CC has come to be known as 'courtesy copy' or 'copy circulated'.

10. Hunting for the response

Something else that is quite annoying is when you have sent a message to someone, and in replying their response is placed at the end of the original message instead of at the top. As a result, you open the e-mail and the first thing you see is your own message, so your first thought is confusion, then it hits you that the sender's message may be somewhere else, so you have to go hunting around looking for the reply. Please don't waste people's time like this. Format your default so your messages are at the top when you click 'Reply'.

When not to use e-mail

There are some situations when you should definitely not use e-mail, and there are other situations when care is needed when drafting your e-mail.

• When messages are confidential

E-mail messages can sometimes be read by other people, certainly by the system administrator if there is one at your organisation. There is also the problem that your recipient could easily forward your message to someone else, perhaps inappropriately. If the information you want to send is very confidential, it would be better to put it in a letter or a memo in an envelope marked as confidential. Alternatively send it as a fax but only if you know the recipient will be at the other end waiting to receive it.

• When messages are long and complicated

E-mail recipients want to process messages quickly, and they usually read messages on-screen. Long, complicated messages do not look good on e-mail. If you really must include a lot of information in an e-mail message, make sure you structure it such that the reader can scan it quickly for essential detail and then study it further when it is more convenient. See my Four Point Plan for structuring e-mail messages in Chapter 6.

• When there are many issues to resolve or clarify

With e-mail there can sometimes be quite a lot of 'to-ing' and 'fro-ing' when an issue has lots of questions to be answered. This can result in lengthy e-mail conversations, which can become quite frustrating. Sometimes it is easier and will save time for everyone if you pick up the telephone to ask questions and receive immediate replies.

• When messages are indiscreet

When you send an e-mail message ask yourself if you would want the message posted on the company notice board, because in essence that's virtually what could happen. E-mail can easily be copied, printed or forwarded. You should never use e-mail to bad-mouth a colleague or employer, to conduct a romantic affair, to pass on gossip or to discuss office politics. The potential for embarrassment is huge, not to mention the possibility of finding yourself out of a job.

Myth Buster

If I send an incriminating, abusive message, I always delete it immediately from my workstation, so no one can find out about it anyway.

Wrong! Your messages could still be hanging around in cyberspace somewhere. Your IT colleagues are most probably backing up your company's mainframe, so anything you say can always come back to haunt you when you least expect it!

• When you are angry

When angry words are written they can be read and reread over and over again as well as forwarded to others and used against you. If you have something unpleasant to discuss with someone, pick up the telephone or discuss it face-to-face. Never use e-mail if you are angry, or your words could come back to haunt you.

• When the message is emotive or sensitive

With the written word there is no body language, intonation or gestures that could help in figuring out the meaning. As such it can be easily misinterpreted and you could quite innocently cause offence to your reader. If the topic is emotive or sensitive, or if your words could be misinterpreted, then don't put it in writing. Such matters are much better dealt with face-to-face so that gestures and tone of voice come into play and your words can be softened as appropriate.

It's always best to put yourself in the other person's position when deciding on the best way to send a message. How will they feel when they read your message? Will your purpose and intent come across clearly, or are misunderstandings possible?

Think twice before you hit 'Send'

Before sending any message think twice before you hit 'Send'. Read it through carefully, as if you were the recipient, and ask yourself:

- Is it easy to read?
- Is my meaning quite clear?
- Is the content hurtful or offensive?
- Is the tone appropriate?
- Is the message right for e-mail?
- Would a letter, a phone call or a face-to-face discussion be better?

 Fast Fact

E-mail is not always the best form of communication. Telephone or face-to-face communication would be more appropriate when:

- You are negotiating.
- You need an instant yes-or-no answer.
- You want to discuss a sensitive or intimate matter.
- You don't want to seem too intimidating.
- You want to retain confidentiality.

 Aha! Moment

I really need to pick up the phone more often!

Turning problems into potential

So now we all have a good understanding of the problems that can occur with e-mail and how we can turn them all around to exploit the full potential of this wonderful communication medium. To end this discussion, here are my five basic rules for fulfilling the great promise of e-mail.

Rule 1: Remember you are talking to a human being

When you are holding a conversation online (and in effect that's what an e-mail exchange is) it's easy for your correspondent to misinterpret your meaning, and vice versa. You can't use facial expressions, gestures or tone of voice to communicate your meanings as you can in a real conversation. Written words are all you have, so make the most of them. Put yourself in the other person's place and imagine how you would feel on receiving that message. While it's good to stand up for yourself, it is important to try not to hurt other people's feelings.

The key here is to think before you click on that 'Send' button. Ask yourself, 'Would I say this to the person's face?' If not, then you must edit, rewrite and reread. Don't send your message until you are quite sure that you would feel just as comfortable saying the words to the person face-to-face.

Rule 2: Make your message clear and to the point

In Chapters 4 and 5 you will learn how to compose effective e-mail messages. The main rule to remember is to make sure your messages are clear and logical. Long-winded words in long-winded sentences will not impress — they will confuse. So pay attention to the content of your writing as well as to the structure and flow of your message. In e-mail we are all judged by one thing alone — the quality of our writing. Learn to love the written word, learn to play with the written word, learn to make the most of the written word. And please: use initial capitals just as you would in a traditional letter, and avoid using hard-to-understand abbreviations, which will only confuse and annoy your reader.

A friend told me that she received a professional enquiry that was written in a very, very casual, almost instant-messenger-like language. This made my friend feel that the sender was not so proficient or respectful, and probably less educated. My friend then called her to discuss the matter rather than e-mail a response, and during their conversation she found the lady to be very pleasant and friendly. My friend decided to tell her the different impression she'd received from her e-mail, and the lady was horrified and very glad of the opportunity to do something about it. Ever since then, her subsequent e-mails have been clear and eloquent, and very effective indeed.

Rule 3: Make your message look good

I know part of the beauty of e-mail is its speed, but how long does it take to write 'Dear Tom' or finish off by writing your name? How long does it take to start a new paragraph every few lines? How long does it take to put a blank line between those paragraphs? Get into these good habits from now on. Looking good online (format and structure) goes hand in hand with sounding good (composition and tone), and these give your reader a good impression of you.

Rule 4: Use the 'Reply' button

Click on 'Reply' when you are responding to someone else's e-mail, rather than simply opening a brand new message to respond to them. Remember, busy people send out dozens of e-mail messages every day. It will help them if you click 'Reply' because the text of their original message will be included in the reply. When you do this, make sure you respond at the top and not at the bottom — there's nothing worse than hunting around for a reply.

Rule 5: Respect your reader's time

Research shows that we all have more work to do and less time to do it. The number of e-mail messages in a person's inbox only adds to this already weighty workload. So show some respect for your reader by keeping your messages brief and concise, including all the relevant details, structuring them logically, using an appropriate salutation and close, and including a clear and specific subject line.

 Aha! Moment

These are not 'rules' at all. They are just common sense principles that will help us to look good, sound good and maximise the great potential of e-mail.

Star Tips for maximising the potential of e-mail

1. Resist the urge to send a rude or abusive message via e-mail — it may come back to haunt you.

2. Keep your messages accurate, brief and concise, and structure them logically.

3. Use an appropriate tone in your messages while considering the reader's feelings.

4. Deal with sensitive issues in person, where gestures and tone of voice can be used to great effect.

5. An important part of your message is communicated by how your e-mail looks. Make sure it looks good.

6. Don't go overboard with CCs. Send copies only to the people who need to know — not to everyone you know!

7. Remember that sometimes the telephone would be a better choice than e-mail.

8. Use the 'Reply' button so that the subject-line (or 'thread') remains identical for the same topic.

9. Remember that it's a human being you're talking to, not a machine.

10. A good gauge when considering language is to ask yourself: 'Would I say this if I was speaking to the reader?'

MANAGING
YOUR MAILBOX

*"Men are only as good as
their technical development
allows them to be."*

George Orwell

3

Some people find the volume of mail in their inbox quite overwhelming. The little beep or voice that comes from their computer, sometimes every few seconds, means that they are constantly being interrupted to see what is in their mailbox. The result of this overwhelming compulsion of e-mail is a real draining effect on your time.

But never fear, help is at hand. All it takes is a little attention to detail and some time management skills. You can regain your power and get some balance back into your working life if you resolve to put e-mail in its place as a tool that can help you, not control you. Throughout this chapter we will discuss tips and techniques to help you to organise your mail, your mailbox and your time.

If e-mail hasn't yet become such an overwhelming burden in your life, beware — it can happen almost overnight! So don't wait until breaking point to implement these time-saving techniques. Start now!

Seven deadly sins of of e-mail management
Read this list of seven deadly sins of e-mail management and tick the ones that apply to you. If you tick a few of these items, you need help. This chapter is just what you need.
1. You deal with work in fragments, jumping from one project to another, from one message to another, without any clear organisation. ☐
2. You click on each message and read it more than once, sometimes several times, before responding. ☐
3. You take on work that should be dealt with by other people instead of forwarding it as appropriate. ☐
4. You retain too many messages in your mailbox without action. ☐
5. You don't answer messages completely so that recipients have to come back for clarification. ☐
6. You don't utilise all the functions of your mailer such as address book, templates and automatic signature. ☐
7. You spend too long every day writing e-mail messages. ☐

'You've got mail' flow chart

This flow chart shows all the basic steps you must go through when you receive mail.

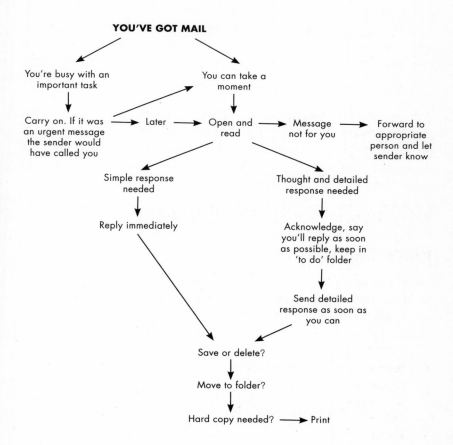

Let's take a look at how best to manage each step of this process.

Receiving mail

'You've got mail!' These words resounding from your computer can be received with a smile or a snarl depending on what sort of day you are having. Some people have their message alert on all the time, so every time they receive a message they are interrupted by a little beep, a flag, a horn, a voice, or even the national anthem! When you are working on an important project, consider switching this off so that you can work uninterrupted. These constant interruptions can really ruin your concentration. Surely nothing can be so important that it can't wait for an hour or two?

A friend of mine said recently, "When I need to concentrate on an important report, I just can't have the alert beeping or popping up all the time, otherwise I wouldn't be able to focus, so I switch off the alert temporarily. This means I can concentrate fully. I get my report finished quicker and it's more likely to be well-written. Then when I've finished, I can concentrate on replying to e-mails to the same effect."

Processing mail

When you are going through your messages, scan each one carefully. Read the subject line and the first paragraph. If necessary scan a little further into the message. Then make a decision whether you will do one of these four things:

1. Save or print it for reading later
2. Delete it
3. Forward it to someone else
4. Act on it

If you leave a message in your inbox with no evaluation at all, it simply means that you will go back to read it again and again. This is just the same as moving pieces of paper around your desk from one tray to another — it is a total waste of time.

When receiving lots of e-mail daily, it's imperative that you quickly read through them all before replying to any, especially when the same exchange involves many different people. An immediate response to an earlier e-mail message may not be the most efficient response based on what may have been mentioned in another message. You can certainly save time and avoid the need for an embarrassed, 'Sorry you're right, I hadn't read that yet' response.

Fast Fact

Don't even bother opening e-mail with subject lines like these:

- Want to Earn Easy $????
- Earn $$$ while you SLEEP!
- Make 1000% on every Sale!

These messages are spam and should be deleted straight away. (See Chapter 9 on spam.)

1. Save for later

Messages that you save may be:

- lower priority
- messages that don't need immediate attention
- for reading only

Make sure you file these messages somewhere you can find them later. Don't leave them in your inbox to be moved around and revisited several times. You may decide to print a message out and put it in a 'reading material' folder to read later (on the train or at home or while waiting for an appointment).

Danger Zone

Don't for one minute think you can just keep your received messages in your inbox and your sent messages in your 'Sent' folder. Organising your mail into folders is essential. Imagine if you were to put all your paper mail into one in-tray without doing any sorting at all. You would quickly reach a point where you cannot find anything at all. Instead, you keep a number of files, each one labelled, so it is easy to file and to find paper mail. The same sort of system applies to e-mail.

2.   Delete it

Unfortunately, we all receive irrelevant messages or junk e-mail (spam), just like we receive junk mail through the post. It's a fact of life. Since you usually throw paper junk mail straight into the wastepaper bin, that's what you do with junk e-mail too. Don't waste any time thinking or worrying about it — just delete it. You can often recognise spam as soon as you see the subject line or the sender's address.

Most e-mail programs have junk mail folders too, so do make sure you check these folders regularly, just in case some legitimate mail lands in there. You may also be able to tag an e-mail as spam so that anything else from the same address will automatically go into your junk folder.

If you find yourself getting a lot of junk mail from a particular party, or are being copied unnecessarily, then you must try to put a stop to it by asking not to be sent any more unwanted information.

3.   Forward it to someone else

If you are not the right person to handle a particular message, then pass it on to someone who is. However, do remember that it's good manners to include a note about why you are sending a particular message. Don't just forward a message without a note. Simply click on 'Forward' and add a few lines — perhaps, 'I think this is your department. Can I pass it over to you?' Also, it's very important to let the sender know where you have forwarded their message and the address of the person they should contact in future.

4. Act on it

Many messages require a simple, straightforward response. If you reply immediately, it's done with and you can forget about it. If you need to give the matter some thought, or do some research first, then put the message in your 'Drafts' folder or highlight the message with the 'Priority' setting, or whatever feature is available on your mailer. It is courteous, however, to send a quick reply first to acknowledge the message and inform the writer that you will get back to them soon. For example:

Hi John

Thanks for your message. I need to check up on a few things before I can reply, so please give me a couple of days and I'll get back to you as soon as I can.

Cheers
Mark

You may need to add this to your written 'Action' list that you keep on your desk (or on your computer) so that you give the matter the relevant priority. When you have all the information necessary to reply, give it the consideration it deserves and reply fully to each point.

Fast Fact

Having a discussion by e-mail is called a 'thread'. Remember to keep the original subject line throughout the e-mail conversation as this helps people to keep track of the thread. Your mailer should allow you to keep all messages with the same subject line together, so it is easy to keep track. If you change the subject midway through a conversation you will not be doing yourself, or the recipient, any favours.

Auto-reply messages

If you are going to be away from the office for any length of time, especially on vacation or public holidays, activate your auto-reply message. In this way all incoming messages will receive an automatic reply and people will not be kept in the dark, wondering why you have not replied. Similarly, auto-responding software enables you to redirect certain messages to other people to handle. This is generally used in larger organisations.

Subject: Auto-reply: Away from office

Thanks for your message. I'm away from the office on a short vacation from 24 to 28 July. For urgent matters, please contact Shamee at shamee@shirleytaylortraining. com or telephone 6838 1069. Otherwise I will respond to you when I return to the office on 29 July.

Many thanks
Shirley

Danger Zone

Please avoid this common mistake seen in many auto-responders:

"*I'm away on course.*"

A ship may be 'on course'.

But you are 'on a course'!

Try This

Edit your own auto-reply message to make sure it looks good and gives a great impression.

Using folders

Given the quantity of e-mails arriving in your inbox, you will find it useful to create a system of folders in which you can file and save the messages you want to keep. You may find it useful to replicate the system of folders you use on your computer when you do this. For example, I use Microsoft Outlook, so in my inbox there are individual folders for each of the trainers that I work with, plus folders for all the companies where I do in-house training. I also have additional folders called: Home, Lawyer, Accountant, etc. I regularly transfer messages to these respective folders, at least once or twice a week. This ensures the folders are always up-to-date when I need to refer to some correspondence.

Using filters (or rules)

It's easy for your inbox to become inundated with incoming mail, especially if you subscribe to automated mailing lists. When you have so much in your inbox it becomes easy to miss the really important messages. Filters help you to deal with this problem. They are sets of rules in your mailer program that you set up so that your mail is sorted into different piles, usually according to the sender and the subject matter. Messages are then filed automatically into the different folders. Some filters will highlight key messages on the incoming mail list with priority codes or colours.

You can easily create a simple filing system by organising your incoming mail into folders — this saves you valuable searching time. Examples of folders include: Work, Personal, Ezines, Articles, To Do. You can also use your e-mail program like a personal organiser, storing draft messages and reminders in your Monday through Sunday or To Do folders.

Your filtering system can be set up to:

- place messages from a mailing list into an appropriate folder so that clutter is removed from your inbox.
- delete unwanted messages.
- reply to messages with a courteous standard response so that correspondents know action is underway.
- detect messages that need special priority so that they sit at the top of your list.

The benefits of being organised

Just like a successful paper management system is a key element in organisational and time-management skills, a good filing system is also the key to successful management of e-mail. With a good filing system you will be able to file messages quickly as well as find them again easily.

Questions to ask yourself about your current filing system are:

- Is your inbox full of messages that are read but not filed?
- Do you have difficulty deciding where to file certain messages?
- Do you have difficulty finding messages again after you have filed them?
- Do you have difficulty identifying messages where action is outstanding?
- Are some folders bulging with mixed messages that should really be broken up into sub-folders?
- Are your folders and sub-folders clearly labelled and easy to access?
- Is the filing system practical and easy to use?

Once you have considered all these factors you will be able to create a mail management system that is much more user-friendly. It may take a few hours to revamp your filing system, especially if radical changes are necessary. But you will see the benefits straight away, with immediate saving in time and frustration.

Subject-based filing systems are most popular with e-mail. You must decide which subjects suit your work, as well as whether sub-categories will be useful within folders. You may also want to create other folders for things like Action, Awaiting Reply, Drafts, etc. Folders will usually be displayed on-screen in alphabetical order. If you want to get something to the top of your list start it with 'AAA' or consider making them sub-folders of a folder called 'Active'. When something is no longer active move it out of this folder into its own named folder. Similarly, anything that you don't need to look at very often (perhaps even personal e-mail if allowed by your company) can be placed at the bottom of the list by starting the folder name with 'ZZZ'.

Try This

Go on! Sort out the folders in your e-mail program now. You know it makes sense.

Star Tips for effective e-mail management

1. Organise your mail into folders with e-mail, just as you do with paper files.

2. Consider turning off your message alert so you can really focus when working on important projects that require concentration.

3. Clear your clutter regularly; this applies to old messages too. Know when to hit 'Delete'.

4. Set up a filing system that is practical for you, using folders and sub-folders. Revamp your filing system regularly to make it as user-friendly as possible.

5. Set up a filter system so that incoming mail is automatically placed in the appropriate folders for ease of reference.

6. Check your 'Sent' messages folder regularly and delete old messages that you do not need to keep.

7. Change your auto-reply every time you use it, to keep the content relevant and current.

8. Keep copies of important messages and consider archiving messages that you may need later.

LOOKING GOOD ONLINE

"There is an invisible garment woven around us from our earliest years; it is made of the way we eat, the way we walk, the way we greet people"

Jean Giraudoux

4

There are six stages we need to go through with every message. In this chapter we'll go through each of these six stages to make sure that you get the details just right in all your e-mail messages.

Tell your mailer that you want to send a new message.

↓

Complete the address line.

↓

Decide if you want to send anyone a copy or a blind copy.

↓

Fill in the subject line.

↓

Compose the message.

↓

Send

Seven deadly sins of message preparation
Read this list of seven deadly sins of message preparation and tick the ones that apply to you. If you tick a few of these items, you need help.

1. You sometimes forget to include a subject heading. At other times you have trouble thinking up an appropriate and relevant heading.	☐
2. You often CC your e-mail messages to lots of people without thinking whether they really need to see them.	☐
3. You sometimes send messages without a greeting or a closing section.	☐
4. You always use the same 'Regards' every time you finish an e-mail.	☐
5. You haven't set up an automatic signature for your e-mail.	☐
6. Your organisation has no standard disclaimer at the end of e-mail messages.	☐
7. You sometimes forget to attach the file you are supposed to attach.	☐

CC and BCC

Use the CC field for the addresses of those people who are not the main recipients of the message but who need to be kept informed. Use the BCC field for sending a blind copy (i.e. without the other recipients knowing about it). Both these features should be used sensibly. Near the top of the list of complaints from the people I surveyed is how it is so easy to click on the CC box and zap off copies of messages to anyone you wish. People who believe their correspondence with you is confidential may not be too happy if they find you've copied their messages to other people, since these may be people they had deliberately left off their original CC list!

Quickly double-check your CC and BCC boxes before you click 'Send'. Make sure they are exactly as you want them to be. It's too easy to hit the wrong key and 'Reply All' so that everyone on the original CC list will receive a copy of your reply.

Fast Fact

For those too young to remember, CC originally stood for 'carbon copy'. Those were the days when we had manual typewriters and backing sheets, and carbon paper was the only way of making duplicate copies of correspondence! Technological evolution has meant that carbon paper is a thing of the past, but CC has stuck — it has now come to mean 'courtesy copy', and BCC 'blind courtesy copy'.

Myth Buster

You feel you need to reply to every e-mail message.

False. Just like real conversations, correspondence via e-mail has natural endings too. If there's no real reason to reply, then don't!

SMART subject lines

Busy business people receive dozens of e-mail messages every day, sometimes hundreds. It is a constant battle to capture the attention and interest of your readers. Too often writers compose subject lines that are far too vague, bland or too long to be effective. If you are guilty of any of these, then you need help with your subject lines.

Do you ever ...	If so ...
leave the subject field blank?	It may be identified as spam and sent to trash.
use a previous e-mail to write about something new, but you leave the old (unrelated) subject line in place?	If you insist on clicking 'Reply' to a previous e-mail when writing about a new topic, please delete all the correspondence and type in the new subject line.
type questions or your whole enquiry in the subject field and leave the message blank?	This is the height of laziness. The subject field is for a subject. The message field is for a message!
type a bland or vague word or phrase in the subject field, which doesn't make it clear what the message is about?	'Hello', 'Enquiry' or 'Latest info' will just not do. Nothing but a clear, concise subject line will do!

Fast Fact

Just like business people prioritise their workload, studies show that e-mail recipients refer to the subject field to prioritise their e-mails, and more importantly, to determine whether or not they will open the e-mail at all. Help your recipient by making it quite clear in your subject line exactly what your message is all about.

If you want to make sure your subject lines stand out from the rest, and so make sure your messages are read, you should aim to make them:

Specific

Meaningful

Appropriate

Relevant

Thoughtful

Specific

Avoid vague or generic subject lines like 'Enquiry' or 'Information'. These are useless.

Meaningful

Make sure your subject line is explicit and meaningful. For example, sending a message to IBM Technical Support with the heading 'Help Needed' is as good as having no heading at all.

Appropriate

Keep your subject line concise and to the point. It should be a brief summary of what the message is about, not an extract from it. It should also be professional and fitting for the purpose.

Relevant

Hit the nail on the head so that the reader is completely clear what you are writing about.

Thoughtful

Spare a thought for readers who may have 50 or more messages in their inbox. By composing a clear, concise subject line you can help both the reader and yourself.

Your subject line should indicate the context of the message at a glance. The length of your subject line may be determined by the e-mail program that you use, but you may be able to adjust the settings. It is a good idea to limit your subject lines to 35–40 characters.

Aha! Moment

What I put in my subject line can often mean the difference between whether my message is read right now, today, tomorrow, next week or never!

Let's take a look at some good and some not-so-good subject lines:

1. This subject line is useless — it tells the reader nothing:

    Subject: Enquiry

    This is more specific, giving the reader an idea of what the message is about:

    Subject: Enquiry about Gold Membership Plan

2. This message is OK but still not specific enough considering the content:

    Subject: Yahoto sale

    This is more meaningful, concise and specific:

    Subject: 27 May — Closing date for Yahoto sale

3. This is rather vague:

    Subject: Quarterly results

    This is much more descriptive:

    Subject: Second quarter results up by 20%

4. This is good, but is the meaning really clear?

    Subject: 10% pay increase for all employees

    You would probably get excited reading that subject line, but if in fact the message was to tell you that you would not be getting a pay increase, then this subject line would be more SMART:

    Subject: Directors reject 10% pay increase

5. Your system may truncate subject lines that are more than a set length. This happens particularly with handhelds. Consider this is what you want to put in your subject field — 'Important information on how to write subject lines that give your e-mail messages some real oomph!' Here's what may appear in your subject field:

    Subject: Important information on how to write sub

    Composing a precise and clear subject line takes practice. In this case, perhaps:

    Subject: Put some oomph into your subject line!

Myth Buster

We should always write in the subject line first, before we write the message.

Says who? It may be better to write your subject line after you've written the message. Then you will be better able to summarise the content more precisely in the subject line.

Danger Zone

It's not OK to hit 'Reply' and keep the same subject heading if you are changing the subject. If you must click on 'Reply', please do two things: (1) change the subject line, and (2) delete the whole history of the previous conversation.

Try This

Take a look in your 'Sent' folder at all your subject headings. Ask yourself if they meet these SMART guidelines.

Greetings (or salutations)

Every new medium develops its own protocols for meeting and greeting as well as for closing. Telephone conversations start with 'Hello' and end with 'Goodbye'. Traditionally, business letters have always followed these golden rules:

Dear Sir
Dear Sirs   } *Yours faithfully*
Dear Madam

Dear John   } *Yours sincerely*
Dear Mrs Smith

These rules are too formal for e-mail messages, but it is still thought to be polite to begin with a greeting. Some people choose to ignore this nicety. They say it's quite clear who the message is to and from because of the automatic headers. However, when no greetings are included, a message can seem cold and the writer somewhat distant. Simple greetings are common courtesy, and this goes a long way. And after all, how long does it take? Are you really too busy to be courteous?

There are two good reasons for including a greeting:

- Readers can double-check that they are the intended recipient when they look at the greeting and see their own name.
- It clarifies the context in which they are receiving the message. For example, if the greeting does not bear your name you should look at the CC list to see if that's the reason why you received the message.

The way you begin your e-mail messages will depend on various factors:

- your relationship with the recipient
- how frequently you communicate with the recipient
- how many recipients there are
- the status of the recipient — you will address your CEO very differently from how you address your colleague in the next office
- your personal style and preference
- your company's preferred style

That said, the way business is conducted in general is much more informal than in the past. Business meetings are much less formal than they used to be. First names are now widely used rather than full formal titles. The same informality is also common in business writing.

If you would greet someone with a first name face-to-face, then do the same in e-mail:

Dear Kelvin

If you would greet someone more formally in person, then do the same in e-mail:

Dear Mr Long

When the recipient replies to you, take a good look at the way he or she signs off at the end of the message. If the recipient has addressed you by your first name and has signed off as 'Ashley Long', then next time you write you may begin with 'Dear Ashley'.

If you are writing to a group of people you can say 'Dear' plus the group name:

Dear Marketing Executives
Dear Supervisors
Dear Manchester United Fans

If you are writing to someone you know very well and/or communicate with regularly, 'Dear' may be a bit too formal. You may want to begin with the more informal 'Hi' or 'Hello':

Hello Mark
Hi Sally

Greetings across cultures

Salutations can be tricky across cultures where sometimes the family name is first and sometimes last, or sometimes there are three or four names and you aren't sure which one you should use when you greet them. It can be frustrating trying to decide on an appropriate greeting in your e-mail, especially if you can't even tell if the person is male or female.

Try This

If you find yourself e-mailing someone whose name you aren't sure about, here are a few suggestions as to what you could do:

- Call up the Consulate for that particular country and ask for their advice.

- Ask a colleague or friend who you know has lived in the country where your reader is from.

- Call up the reception of the person's company and ask them how to address this person.

- Call up the person him/herself, introduce yourself, and ask them how you should address them. This personal contact will definitely go a long way towards building better bonds even before you e-mail them. Learn more about building better relationships in Chapter 7.

Fast Fact

Greetings like 'Good Morning' or 'Good Afternoon' don't really make much sense with e-mail. You never know when your recipient will open his or her mail, especially when communicating across time zones.

Ending your message

Once again there are mixed feelings about how to finish an e-mail message. The jury is still out regarding appropriate closes for e-mail — at least my jury is. I have never been a great fan of the word 'Regards', which I hate to see at the foot of letters, memos and faxes. It seems so cold and unemotional, even quite terse. However I can see that in e-mail this is one of the most popular closings, so on this issue I have to hold my hands up and submit. So if you feel comfortable with it, go ahead and end your e-mail messages with 'Regards', but don't expect to receive a message from me with that ending!

If it suits your personality, for more informal messages or with people you know really well, you may choose something like:

Cheers

If you have been writing to ask someone to do something it may be appropriate to finish with:

Many thanks

On some occasions a close with a little more feeling may be appropriate:

Best wishes
All the best
Good luck!
See you soon

Here are some other popular closings:

Best
Yours
Warmly
Take care

You could also end with phrases that reflect the purpose of your e-mail, in which case you really don't need anything else, such as:

Have a great day.
Enjoy your weekend.
Happy Holidays!
To your success.
Keep up the good work.

Fast Fact

Your closing is really just the icing on the cake. Your main message is what will really set the whole tone of your message, so that's the most important section. But by choosing an appropriate sign-off, you are giving just one more sign of what a great pleasure it's going to be communicating with you.

Signatures

There are two good reasons for a sign-off section:

- Without a sign-off your recipient will have no other information about you except your e-mail address. If you have included a sign-off or signature, then your recipient will be able to address you correctly.

- A sign-off section lets your recipient know that they have reached the end of your message. It is not uncommon for e-mail transmissions to be interrupted, so at least if you have signed off appropriately you know your reader will not be left wondering, 'Is that all?'

Include your job title, the name of your organisation and contact details. Telephone numbers are particularly important things to include because the recipient may actually want to discuss the matter with you verbally. Do remember that whenever any of the details change you must revise your signature details to ensure everything is up-to-date.

Here's a detailed signature:

Shirley Taylor
CEO, ST Training Solutions Pte Ltd

 ST Training Solutions

391B Orchard Road, 13-09 Ngee Ann City Tower B
Singapore 238874
Tel: +65 6838 1069   Fax: +65 6722 0739
Company website: www.shirleytaylortraining.com
Shirley's website: www.shirleytaylor.com
ASSAP website: www.shirleytaylortraining.com/ASSAP

For people who know you better and have all your details, or for personal e-mails, you may want to include your personal contact details or a website address:

Shirley Taylor
Website: www.shirleytaylor.com
Telephone +65 6838 1069

 Myth Buster

People expect to see advertising messages and images too as part of your signature file.

Not necessarily! Don't make the mistake of thinking that everyone wants to read another entire paragraph of your ad material. Keep your signature file short with essentials only. Don't scare people off with too much information.

Final thoughts on greetings and closings

In one of my workshops, a man was very adamant that he didn't need to use a greeting or a closing. "You know it's for you, it's in your mailbox. You know it's from me, it says so! I finish all my messages with 'Cheers' and nothing else." We couldn't make him agree that he needed his name at the end, so we just moved on. The second morning he walked into the room laughing, and told me, "Shirley, I have a lot of correspondence from Japan, and last night I opened my mail and one message began, 'Dear Mr Cheers'." I think from that day onwards, this man has always put his name at the end of messages!

Disclaimers and confidentiality clauses

Whether your e-mail messages should include a disclaimer and/or confidentiality notice is a matter that must be considered by companies individually. From a legal point of view it may be advisable to do so. Some companies have different disclaimers for internal and external messages, but what may begin as an internal message may be copied externally. This must be considered when composing disclaimer notices.

Here are some examples of disclaimers:

> *This e-mail is confidential and intended for the addressee only. If you are not the person to whom it is addressed, you must not print, copy or distribute it or take any action on it. E-mail may be intercepted or corrupted and XYZ Company is unable to accept responsibility for any breach of confidence arising through use of this medium. XYZ Company will not accept liability for contractual commitments or statements made by individuals employed by this company outside the scope of our business.*

> *XYZ Company does not accept legal responsibility for the contents of this message. Any views or opinions presented are solely those of the author and do not necessarily represent those of XYZ Company.*

> *This e-mail may be confidential and privileged. Any form of unauthorised use is prohibited. If it has been wrongly sent to you, please delete it immediately and notify the sender.*

Fast Fact

Disclaimers are becoming more and more complex. But keep in mind that legally they offer only limited protection, no matter how long and complicated they are!

Attachments

One of the most useful features of e-mail is the ability to attach files. This allows people to share any file in any format — Word documents, JPEG-encoded images, Photoshop files, Excel spreadsheets, PowerPoint presentations, audio/visual files, data files, and so on. If something can be saved as an electronic file, it can be sent along with any e-mail message. This works very well when:

- you remember to attach the file.
- your reader has the software that is compatible with yours.
- the attachment does not contain a virus.

 Danger Zone

I'm sure you've been guilty more than once of sending an e-mail without the attachment, so you have to send another one saying "Oops, I forgot to attach this." This is a common and easily made mistake, but it can be annoying if it happens too often. Why not make a point to attach the file before you start typing the message? Alternatively when you type the part of the message that says the file is attached, stop immediately and attach the file. This works for me.

Frustration can occur with attachments, especially when your correspondent cannot open the file. One of the main reasons for this is that the recipient does not have the same version of the software that you use. If this happens you can often spend ages sending e-mail back and forth saying, 'It didn't work — can you try sending it again?' Before sending a file, if you are in any doubt at all it's best to send a simple e-mail asking if the recipient can accept attachments easily.

When sending an attachment, bear in mind that it may lose some of its format when viewed by your recipient. This has happened to me on numerous occasions when, for example, I have prepared materials for a presentation and the recipient doesn't have the fonts that I have used. As a result your document can end up looking quite different at the receiving end.

Zip it up

Downloading large files can sometimes take a long time as well as take up a lot of space. Software is available that automatically compresses files (e.g. WinZip or StuffIt) but you will need to ensure that your recipient has the software necessary to decompress them at the other end. WinZip also allows you to send as many files as you want to attach as one single compressed file.

Post the attachment instead

An alternative to attaching files to e-mails is to post the file on an intranet server and tell your recipients where the file can be found. The recipients can then decide if and when they actually want to look at it, and then whether or not they will download it onto their own workstation. This can be particularly useful, for instance, when you inform members about a staff meeting. You can post all the presentation materials on your website, then send a message to all participants with the URL (and possibly the password if the documents are confidential). They can then download whatever documents they need or want.

 Myth Buster

Sending a 'Recall Last Message' e-mail will stop people reading your mail.

Sorry! Sending people an e-mail asking them not to read the e-mail you just sent them is an invitation for them to read it. Get your message right by checking it carefully before you hit 'Send'!

Star Tips for looking good online

1. If you want to ensure your message is opened and read, a SMART subject line is essential.

2. Always include an appropriate greeting and closing section on all your messages.

3. Use automatic signatures and change them when appropriate.

4. Don't be tempted to click 'Reply All', and do CC only the people who really need to know.

5. Remember to include some niceties at the end of messages, such as 'Good luck', 'Have a great weekend', etc.

6. Attachments are great, but only when you remember to attach them.

7. Remember, e-mail conversations come to an end too.

WRITING GREAT E-MAILS

"Those who write clearly have readers, those who write obscurely have commentators."

Abraham Lincoln

Having taken such a lot of trouble to ensure that all your preliminary work is done correctly, it would be a shame to fall down at the most important hurdle. Your message is the most important part, so you need to make sure you say what you want to say in straightforward modern business language and appropriate tone, and make sure it looks good. That way it has a greater chance of being effective.

Effective communication gives a professional impression of you and your organisation and helps to get things done. It seems we are now writing more than ever, and very often speed is the key to successful negotiations. Writing effectively under these circumstances can be very challenging.

In this chapter we will be looking at ways in which you can improve your written communication, even in the most demanding circumstances, so that your messages are effective and achieve the desired results.

Seven deadly sins of business writing	
Read this list of seven deadly sins of business writing and tick the ones that apply to you. If you tick a few of these items, you need help. This chapter will help you write great e-mails that get the right results.	
1. You use language in business communication that is more suited to your great-grandparents.	☐
2. You use lots of old-fashioned or unnecessary words and expressions just because other people always use them.	☐
3. You spend a lot of time thinking of what to say and trying to get your messages just right.	☐
4. You have long e-mail conversations back and forth with people trying to clarify things and answer more questions.	☐
5. You write brief messages that sometimes come over as cold and unfeeling.	☐
6. You don't know the difference between active and passive voice.	☐
7. Some people tell you that your tone in e-mails is very abrupt.	☐

Traditional versus modern business writing

I regularly conduct workshops teaching people how to write effective letters and e-mails, and I'm always amazed at how many young people still use so many old-fashioned expressions. Why is this? On the one hand we keep up-to-date with new technology, new computer programs and software. Yet on the other hand we often use language and expressions more suited to our great-grandparents. Such an irony!

Not too many decades ago, business writing was formal, long-winded, pompous and serious. Take a look at this letter, which may have been written a few decades ago. Go through it and highlight all the old-fashioned phrases and outdated words. Also look out for passive phrases and redundancies.

Dear Sir,

We have received your letter dated 27th March.

We are extremely distressed to learn that an error was made pertaining to your esteemed order. The cause of your complaint has been investigated, and it actually appears that the error occurred in our packing section, but it was not discerned before the order was despatched to your goodself.

Kindly be informed that arrangements have been made for a repeat order to be despatched to you immediately, and this should leave our warehouse later today.

Enclosed herewith please find a copy of our new catalogue for your reference and perusal.

Should you have any further queries, please do not hesitate to contact the undersigned.

Thank you for your kind attention.

Yours faithfully,
Zachariah Creep & Partners

If you were looking for all the points I asked you to look for, virtually the entire letter would be highlighted by now. The way business is conducted has changed immensely over the last few decades, even more so in the last few years. Informality is now the key. Writing styles have also changed tremendously. The aim in modern business communication is to write in a friendly, informal style using plain language, as if you are having a conversation. See how different today's approach is:

Dear Mr Tan

YOUR ORDER NUMBER TH3456

Thank you for your letter dated 27 March.

I am very sorry about the mistake with your order. This error happened in our packing section, and unfortunately it was not noticed before the goods were sent to you.

A repeat order will be sent to you immediately. It should leave our warehouse today.

Once again, my apologies for the inconvenience.

I enclose our latest catalogue, which I'm sure you will find interesting.

Please call me on 6454545 if you have any questions.

Yours sincerely

Lena Cheng

Did you spot the difference in the second one? Did you notice the short sentences and active phrases instead of passive ones, simple words instead of lengthy ones, and the absence of redundancies and old-fashioned phrases?

You will not develop your own writing style overnight. Practise the skills of choosing words and constructing sentences and paragraphs. Take pride in your work and seek ways to improve it constantly. Learn how to be critical and notice when something is well written and when it is badly written. Find a mode of expression that suits you.

What goes wrong in written communication?

I'm sure we must all have received written communication that failed to achieve its objectives. Whether it's e-mail, letters, memos or faxes, have you ever received any communication that failed in these areas?

- Your gender is changed to Mr instead of Mrs or Miss.
- The purpose of the message is not clearly stated.
- The response required is not clearly stated.
- The message is all jumbled up with no thought given to structure.
- The writer uses long sentences and long paragraphs that look uninviting.
- The message is full of long-winded jargon and redundancies.
- The tone is wrong — sharp, critical, patronising or intimidating.
- Vital details are missing, so you have to send another message to clarify.

Why do these problems happen? One reason is that, as a sender, you are not there physically to help to put your message across with body language, gestures, facial expressions, tone of voice and your personality. Some other reasons are:

- It takes time to write and to reply. Some messages need more thought than others to work out exactly what you want or need to say.
- You may be trying to think up too many words that will look impressive.

- If your thinking is muddled, the structure of your message will be muddled too.
- If you are thinking as you write, sometimes you will waffle and your writing can become unclear and confusing.

All these problems can be improved with experience, with constant awareness, and by taking a sincere interest in the way you write.

 Try This

Next time you are tempted to write these phrases, change them as shown here:

Instead of	Write
Appreciate if you would ...	Please ...
Please be reminded...	Please remember ...
The above-mentioned order ...	This order ...
Please find attached ...	I am attaching ...

The ABC of modern business writing

In every message you write, your aim should be to ensure that every message is:

Accurate

Brief

Clear

Accuracy

Your message should be factually correct in every detail. Make sure you double-check dates, times, names and numbers. Accuracy also means coming straight to the point and being specific. Make sure the reader is aware of all the facts and that nothing is omitted. For example:

Instead of	Write
My flight arrives at 1.30.	My flight BA10 arrives at 1330 on Monday 7 October.
I want to complain about the bad service I received when I visited your store recently.	I was very unhappy about the service I received when I was in your Shoe Department at 1030 on Thursday 7 November.

Brevity

Busy business people welcome messages that are direct and to the point. Save the recipient's time by keeping sentences short and simple, and by avoiding long-winded, old-fashioned jargon. For example:

Instead of	Write
Please be informed that this order will be despatched to you on 12 July.	This order will be sent out on 12 July.
I am writing to inform you that regretfully I am unable to accept your invitation to your opening on this particular occasion.	I'm sorry I cannot attend your opening.
Should you require any further clarification please do not hesitate to contact me.	Please give me a call if you have any questions.
As per our discussion, I will accordingly speak to my colleague Jonathan Long and request that he sends you our quotation as soon as possible.	My colleague, Jonathan Long, will send you our quotation soon.
We seek your assistance to forward to us the additional premium of S$15.62 at your earliest convenience. Kindly note that payment should reach us by 28 November 2009.	Please let us have your cheque for S$15.62 by 28 November 2009.

Clarity

Use everyday language that the reader will understand. Keep words plain and simple rather than using fancy words and elaborate phrases. For example:

Instead of	Write
commence	start
despatch	send
ascertain	find out
attempt	try
accordingly	so, therefore
terminate	end
prior to	before
come to a decision	decide
give consideration to	consider
in the event that	if

 Danger Zone

Some of my workshop participants tell me their bosses expect them to use long words and flamboyant expressions because they will impress their readers. This can't be further from the truth. Readers will soon get bored with such verbosity and will stop reading.

Our great-grandfathers used very long-winded, almost bombastic words many decades ago, but this is certainly not appropriate for the 21st century. Today's writing must be straightforward, simple, brief, and courteous — but definitely not flamboyant!

Benefits of the ABC approach

By using the ABC approach in all your writing, you will:

- **Save time.** Your reader will not have to think about what you mean. It will be crystal clear.
- **Avoid confusion.** Your reader will know exactly what you are saying and the response needed without having to send you an e-mail message or give you a call to clarify anything.
- **Create a good impression.** A well-written message will make the reader think well not only of you but also of your organisation.
- **Enhance relationships.** You will establish a good relationship with people with whom you communicate regularly.
- **Achieve the desired results.**

Remember, high standards in an organisation's business correspondence suggest high standards in business generally.

Myth Buster

We can use capitals to emphasise important sections of our e-mail messages.

Please don't. Apart from being more difficult to read, capital letters imply shouting and aggression. SO DON'T USE CAPITALS FOR ANY PART OF YOUR MESSAGE! also pls don't use lower case letters with abbreviations n acronyms. If u write this way u r thot of as lazy and I 4 one wouldn't want that, wld u?

Six rules of good writing

As well as this ABC approach, it is important to know some of the fundamental rules of good writing. Here is what you need to remember when writing any business documents, not just e-mails:

Rule 1: Avoid redundant phrases

A lot of messages are filled with long-winded jargon, which has no place in modern business language:

For example:

☒ *Please be informed that a management meeting will be held on Monday 12 July 2010.*
☑ *A management meeting will be held on Monday 12 July 2010.*

Try This

Throw these expressions in your trash bin:

☒ *I would like to advise you that ...*

☒ *I would like to bring to your attention that ...*

☒ *I would like to take this opportunity to ...*

☒ *I would like to inform you that ...*

☒ *Thank you for your kind attention.*

☒ *Thank you in anticipation.*

Rule 2: Create KISSable messages

The essence of good business writing is to keep it to the essentials. Busy business people don't have time to read long rambling messages anyway. Say what you want to say in the quickest possible way, while retaining courtesy of course.

When composing e-mail messages make sure you remember your KISSing skills:

Keep

It

Short and

Simple

KISS means simplify your words and phrases as in these examples:

Instead of	Write
utilise	use
purchase	buy
visualise	see
assist	help
sufficient	enough
succeed in making	make
in view of the fact that	as, since
conduct an investigation	investigate
We would like to ask you to	Please

Keeping it short and simple also means avoiding unnecessary words and expressions. There are many frequently-used words that add nothing to the message. These words could easily be removed without changing the meaning. Here are some words and phrases to cut out of your writing:

Unnecessary words and phases	
absolutely	in other words
actually	in the end
all things being equal	in the final analysis
as a matter of fact	in this connection
at the end of the day	in view of the fact that
at this moment in time	I would like to take this opportunity
basically	last but not least
currently	each and every one
in due course	the fact of the matter is
obviously	to all intents and purposes

Rule 3: Use modern terminology

Today's business language should be as natural as possible, as if you were having a conversation. Here are some examples of old-fashioned business jargon that has been updated to a more natural, conversational style:

Instead of	Write
Referring to your message of 23 May.	Thanks for your message of 23 May.
Attached herewith please find ...	Attached is ... I attach ... I am attaching ... Here is ...
Please advise me ...	Please let me know ...
I should be grateful if you would be good enough to advise me ...	Please let me know ...
Please favour us with a prompt reply.	I look forward to your prompt reply.
Should you require any further clarifications please do not hesitate to contact me.	Please give me a call if you have any questions.

Rule 4: Touch up your tone

When speaking to someone face-to-face, it's easy to alter your tone of voice to convey messages in different ways. Much of what you say is also interpreted through non-verbal clues — eye contact, gestures, voice intonation, etc.

This is not possible with the written word, so good business writers learn to choose their words very carefully. It is so important to get the tone right because using the wrong tone could cause real offence to your reader and could lose you an important business contact — or friend.

Tone can help to make a message sound firm or friendly, persuasive or conciliatory, helpful or condescending, according to the impression you wish to convey. Here are some irritating expressions that you should avoid in your writing:

YOUR NEGLECT

IT IS NOT OUR FAULT

YOU SHOULD KNOW

YOUR REFUSAL TO CO-OPERATE

YOU FAILED TO

WE CANNOT BE EXPECTED TO

YOU CANNOT EXPECT

WE MUST INSIST

When writing in business analyse these four important factors and adopt an appropriate tone that reflects them all:

- your status
- the status of the recipient
- your relationship with the recipient
- the content of the message

Consider the way these expressions come across, and study the better way:

☒ *We cannot do anything about your problem. Try calling an electrician.* (too abrupt)

☑ *I am sorry that we cannot help with this. I believe an electrician would be better able to help with this type of work.*

☒ *Your interview will be held on Wednesday 28 August at 1400 hours (too bossy and unfeeling)*

☑ *I hope you can attend an interview on Wednesday 28 August at 2 pm.*

☒ *Your computer's guarantee has expired, so you will have to pay for it to be repaired. (too blunt)*

☑ *The guarantee for your computer has expired, so unfortunately there will be a charge for this.*

☒ *Problems of this type are quite common with the cheaper model. Next time I suggest you spend a bit more money. (too condescending)*

☑ *Problems of this type are far less common with the more advanced model.*

☒ *Our phone bills are enormously high. Please stop making so many personal calls. (too emotive and sharp)*

☑ *The company's telephone bills have increased considerably. Please help by avoiding non-urgent personal calls.*

 Danger Zone

If you write a message in anger, avoid the temptation of hitting 'Send' straight away. Instead, leave it in your 'Drafts' folder for at least an hour. Go make a cup of coffee, do a few other jobs, do some deep breathing if necessary, then go back and look at your e-mail again. Chances are, you will want to tone it down a bit!

Rule 5: Consider your reader

Empathy is an important quality to remember in all business dealings. This is particularly so when sending e-mail messages. When reading through your e-mail before sending it, make sure you empathise with your reader. This means imagining how they will feel as they read your message. Ask yourself these questions:

- Will the reader find your message clear and well written?
- Have you written confidently and positively?
- Have you obtained the right balance between formality and informality while retaining courtesy?
- Will they be confused, annoyed or feel that you have wasted their time?
- Does your e-mail convey a good impression?
- Is the language appropriate or over their head?
- Could anything be considered insensitive or distasteful?

When you have put yourself in the reader's shoes and considered your message carefully, it may be necessary to reword the message more appropriately or restructure it so that it achieves a smooth transition from one idea to the next.

 Danger Zone

Be very obvious with your meanings in e-mail, since subtleties can often be lost or completely misunderstood. Remember this too when reading other people's e-mail. Their understanding of the language, or their haste in composing the e-mail, may have given it a 'tone' that can easily come across as being derogatory or aggressive. Reread it and see if you are simply misinterpreting the words.

Rule 6: If you wouldn't say it, don't write it

The golden rule of writing today is to write as you would speak. Ask yourself how you would say something if you were face-to-face with your correspondent. Take a look at these expressions that are often used in written communication, and consider how they can be improved by using a more conversational style.

☒ *We have received your e-mail.*
☑ *Thanks for your message.*

☒ *The above-mentioned seminar will be held on 15 July, Saturday.*
☑ *This seminar will be held on Saturday 15 July.*

☒ *The below-mentioned goods will be despatched to you next week.*
☑ *These goods will be sent to you next Tuesday.*

☒ *The list of CDs for which we need replacements are as below-mentioned.*
☑ *Here is the list of CDs that we need you to replace.*

☒ *Please do not hesitate to contact the below-mentioned staff if you have any further questions.*
☑ *Please give me a call if you have any questions.*

☒ *Please furnish me with this information soonest.*
☑ *I hope you can let me have this information soon.*

 Myth Buster

Many of my workshop participants say to me, "Shirley, I use a very informal style when I'm speaking to people, but when I write to them I have to use a more formal style, right?"

Wrong! It's the 21st century and we need to write as though we are speaking for it to sound natural; not in a fake, false way that takes too much effort and sounds totally insincere.

Compose CLEAR messages

You can ensure your e-mail messages are effective if you follow these CLEAR guidelines:

Compact

Logical

Empathetic

Action-based

Right

Compact

Einstein once said, 'Everything should be as simple as possible, but no simpler.' Keep your message brief and concise, with short sentences, in straightforward conversational language. This will be easier for you to write and for your readers to read and understand.

Logical

Remember that all good messages begin with an opening, then continue with the main details, and lead naturally to an action statement. (Check out my Four Point Plan in Chapter 6.)

Empathetic

Respect your readers, identify with them, appreciate their feelings. In this way you will ensure that your message is written in words they will understand and in an appropriate tone.

Action-based

Explain exactly what you want your readers to do or how you wish them to respond, then they are more likely to do so.

Right

Make sure your message is correct in terms of grammar, spelling and punctuation, and that it includes all essential facts and details.

 Myth Buster

Many people tell me that following these 'keep it simple' guidelines is one thing when you are just writing simple messages, but they find that keeping messages short and simple can easily come across as blunt and abrupt. Is it possible to be brief but still retain courtesy? With effort, yes. You will find lots of examples of this in Chapter 7.

Do you down-edit?

Some conversations on e-mail can become quite lengthy. I hit 'Reply', then you hit 'Reply', then I reply, then you, etc etc. As such, messages can become very long. Do take a few moments every now and again to down-edit your messages by removing anything that's not necessary to the clarity of the ongoing conversation. I do this regularly to get rid of things like e-mail headers, signature files, and disclaimers that are repeated at the bottom of messages.

However, down-editing can also involve removing any part of the sender's e-mail that is not necessary to the clarity of the ongoing conversation, and then interspersing your comments with those of the sender. Take a look at this example taken from e-mail correspondence with a friend.

As you can see here, the recipient (Alison) has cut away some of the received e-mail, leaving just the paragraphs that she wants to comment on. After this, she hits the 'Enter' key twice and then continues with her comments. She then continues in this way throughout the e-mail, and finishes off with an appropriate close.

With some e-mail programs you will find > at the beginning of each line that was in your original message. Some people like this, because they know any line not beginning with this symbol is your reply. Others find it confusing especially when the same font and colour is used for both the recipient's and your comments.

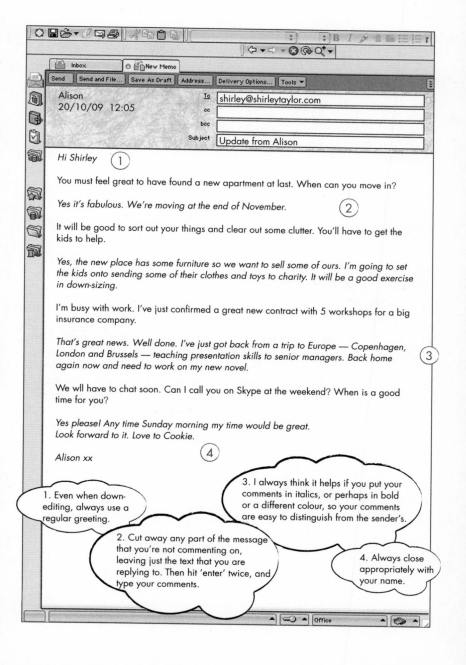

1. Even when down-editing, always use a regular greeting.

2. Cut away any part of the message that you're not commenting on, leaving just the text that you are replying to. Then hit 'enter' twice, and type your comments.

3. I always think it helps if you put your comments in italics, or perhaps in bold or a different colour, so your comments are easy to distinguish from the sender's.

4. Always close appropriately with your name.

To be honest, I am only a fan of this method of down-editing if all my original message is retained, and if the sender's comments are highlighted in a different colour. I find it quite confusing if the other person cuts away a big portion of my message, because I will have to refer to my original message if I want to remind myself what I wrote. I find it more useful to have the whole conversation on both sides in the message.

However, I do find that interspersing comments in this way is most helpful in lengthy dialogues, and particularly in negotiations, when my original comments are in black, then the recipient replies in blue, then I reply in purple, then the recipient in green, etc. However, some people don't like all these colours because different colours evoke different emotions in each of us. You have to figure out what works for you and your recipient.

 Try This

Do try down-editing for yourself. What's good for some will not be good for others. In general, I think this method is more appropriate when e-mailing friends rather than in business e-mail. I also must add that no matter what form of down-editing you use, a greeting and a close are essential.

Star Tips for writing great e-mails

1. Learn the difference between modern business language and old-fashioned jargon.

2. Come straight to the point in messages while retaining courtesy and clarity.

3. Remember the KISS principle in all your written messages. Keep it short and simple.

4. Consider the other person's feelings and make sure you use appropriate tone in your messages.

5. Remember your ABC. Accuracy, Brevity and Clarity will save time, avoid confusion, create a good impression and enhance relationships.

6. Write as if you are having a conversation with the recipient, using everyday language that you would use if you were speaking.

7. Make sure all your e-mail messages are CLEAR: Compact, Logical, Empathetic, Action-based, and Right.

8. If an e-mail exchange is getting rather long and complicated, it may be more effective to pick up the telephone.

PLANNING AND STRUCTURING YOUR MESSAGES

"Plan your work for today and every day, then work your plan."

Norman Vincent Peale

6

Any writing is best tackled systematically, using an approach that ensures a logical flow. There are many things you need to think about before you even start putting your fingers on the keyboard. And when you've finished the document, you must not hit 'Send' until you are quite sure it's all good to go.

A well-structured document written in good business language is the key to effective communication. This chapter will help you to get past that blank page and start creating well-structured documents that will get the right results.

Seven deadly sins of planning and structuring your messages
Read this list of seven deadly sins and tick the ones that apply to you. If you tick a few of these items, you need help. This chapter will provide all the guidance you need.
1. You sometimes don't know where to start a message, and your fingers sit on the keyboard for ages wondering how to begin. ☐
2. You get straight to the point in some e-mail messages, without considering an appropriate opening to lead in nicely. ☐
3. You use unnatural phrases to open your messages, like "We spoke" or "As spoken" or "This refers to your message." ☐
4. You think it's acceptable to write your entire message in one paragraph. ☐
5. Your recipients sometimes write back asking you to clarify certain points from your e-mail. ☐
6. You don't think it's important to reflect for a moment before you begin an e-mail to ask yourself what's the purpose of your message. ☐
7. You don't organise your thoughts before you start writing, and then you wonder why writing is so difficult. ☐

Seven steps to success in planning messages

Here's a formula that will help you to PRODUCE first-class e-mail messages:

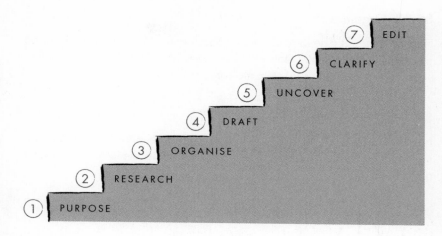

Step 1: Purpose

Ask yourself lots of questions before you start writing:

- Why am I writing this message?
- What do I want to achieve?
- What are my objectives?
- Why am I writing?
- How will I get the right results?

Step 2: Research

You wouldn't start baking a cake unless you had all the ingredients, would you? So it is with writing. Gather all the information together that will help you get your message across. Ask yourself:

- What does the reader know already?
- What will help the reader to understand?
- What important details do I need to give?
- What will the reader's attitude be?

Step 3: Organise

Here is where you need to sort your ideas out in a logical order. I will be discussing my Four Point Plan with you soon, which will help you structure your messages in a very systematic way.

Step 4: Draft

Now you are ready to put your fingers on the keyboard and draft your message, remembering all the points discussed in the previous chapter of course.

 Danger Zone

This is the point at which may people hit 'Send'! It will never be the right thing to do, and may be a big mistake. Don't hit 'Send' until you have satisfied yourself that you have gone through all seven steps in this model.

Step 5: Uncover the reader's reaction

This is probably the most important step. It's where you take off your head and put on the head of the reader. Ask yourself:

- Are all the facts and figures correct?
- Have I missed anything out, or included anything irrelevant?
- Will the reader understand everything, or will clarification be necessary?
- Is the action stated clearly?
- Is the message clear, concise, courteous and complete?

Step 6: Clarify

If you are not completely happy with your draft, you must make some changes to clarify your message. Improve the structure, the tone, the choice of words. Keep the reader and your objectives in mind.

Step 7: Edit

Once again, go through your document with a fine-tooth comb. Check for grammar, spelling, and punctuation, and then check again.

Aha! Moment

Once I get into the habit of going through this seven step procedure, it will become automatic and like second nature to me. I will reap the rewards.

The Four Point Plan for structuring messages logically

Many e-mail messages are short and routine. They can often be written without any special preparation. However, others may take more thought and planning.

When I ask people what goes wrong in e-mails, one of the most common complaints is that they find it difficult to focus when reading a message that's all jumbled up and badly structured. Busy business people don't want to have to hunt all over the place for the most important details in an e-mail message. They need everything written in a logical order, with the action stated clearly and simply.

I've been teaching this Four Point Plan for many years, and I'm sure it's one of the keys to writing effectively. Let's take a quick glimpse at each of these four sections of this Four Point Plan, and then we'll look in more detail at each section:

Opening	Think of this as the background and basics. This is where you set the scene. You may refer to a telephone conversation, an e-mail, a meeting, an enquiry.	Keep this section short. Just set the scene.
Details	Think of this as all the facts and figures. Give all the information (or ask for it). Provide all relevant details. Use short paragraphs with a space between each.	The longest section of your message. Make sure it flows logically.
Action	This is where you tell the reader the response you want. You may sometimes begin with a conclusion.	What do you want the reader to do next?
Closing	Usually a simple one-line sentence to finish off.	Make it relevant.

Openings

The opening section of an e-mail seems to be one that causes the most difficulty for writers. People tell me they put their fingers on the keyboard and often don't know where to start. As a result, openings can often become very stilted and artificial. Remember, it's here you want to create a real bond with your reader, so use friendly, modern sentences instead of the wooden and unnatural phrases that we see so often:

Instead of	Write
As spoken ...	Thanks for your call this morning.
We spoke.	It was great to speak to you.
We received your message.	Thanks for your message.
	Thank you for your e-mail.
	It was good to hear from you today.
This follows our meeting earlier.	It was good to meet you this morning.
	Thank you for your time this morning.
Your order was received today.	Many thanks for your order.
We are organising a conference for secretaries on 12 November 2010.	ST Training Solutions is proud to invite you to our exciting conference for secretaries in November.

 Try This

If you are often stuck on how to begin your e-mail, think about your aim. Is it:

- to alert a manager to a problem?
- to request details and information?
- to notify someone about a meeting?
- to persuade a manager to increase your budget?

Mention this key point in the first paragraph and it should then be easier to elaborate with all the essential details.

Details

This will be the central and longest part of your message. Think of it as the meat in your sandwich. It is where you give all the new information, or reply to the reader's queries. This is where you will include the facts and figures, giving all the information the reader needs. Remember to separate this section into paragraphs where appropriate, with one line space between each. You may have to restructure this part before you finalise your message, so that you ensure all the details flow nicely in a logical order.

Action

This section may begin with a conclusion. For example, in a letter of complaint you may begin this section with "I am very disappointed with the way I was treated." You will then proceed by stating what action you expect the reader to take, or what you will do next, for example:

I hope you will investigate this situation and take the necessary action.

Please complete the attached reply form and return it to me by 12 July.

I would like your report by next Monday 21 October.

Our Customer Service Manager, Mr James Tan, will contact you soon to arrange an appointment to meet you.

Closings

You can often ruin an e-mail with a boring close, so always make sure you finish off with something relevant and thoughtful.

Instead of	Write
Please revert to me at your soonest.	I hope to hear from you soon.
Your prompt reply would be appreciated.	I look forward to your prompt reply.
Please do not hesitate to contact me should you require any further information.	Please call me if you have any questions.
Please feel free to contact me if you need further assistance.	Please let me know if you need any help.

Myth Buster

We should always finish our messages with "Thank you."

Thank you for what? For reading your message? Forget it. If you have been courteous in your message, no one will ever miss a boring "Thank you" at the end. So drop it, unless you say thank you for something, for example:

- *Thank you for your help.*

- *Thank you for your patience.*

- *Thanks for your understanding.*

- *Thanks for all your support.*

Aha! Moment

We should write as we speak, casually and conversationally. And when someone has done something, thank them for it!

The Four Point Plan in practice

Study these examples of well-structured e-mails:

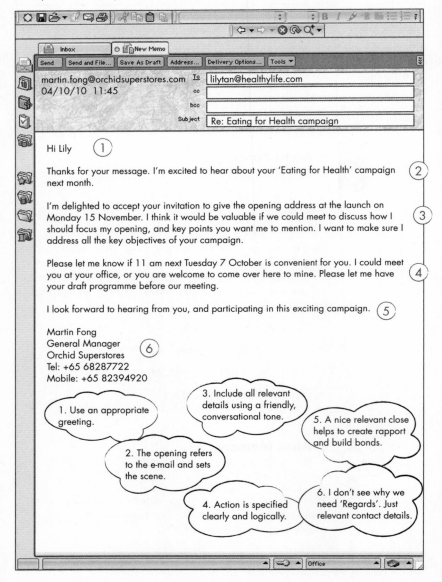

martin.fong@orchidsuperstores.com   To: lilytan@healthylife.com
04/10/10 11:45

Subject: Re: Eating for Health campaign

Hi Lily   (1)

Thanks for your message. I'm excited to hear about your 'Eating for Health' campaign next month.   (2)

I'm delighted to accept your invitation to give the opening address at the launch on Monday 15 November. I think it would be valuable if we could meet to discuss how I should focus my opening, and key points you want me to mention. I want to make sure I address all the key objectives of your campaign.   (3)

Please let me know if 11 am next Tuesday 7 October is convenient for you. I could meet you at your office, or you are welcome to come over here to mine. Please let me have your draft programme before our meeting.   (4)

I look forward to hearing from you, and participating in this exciting campaign.   (5)

Martin Fong
General Manager   (6)
Orchid Superstores
Tel: +65 68287722
Mobile: +65 82394920

1. Use an appropriate greeting.

2. The opening refers to the e-mail and sets the scene.

3. Include all relevant details using a friendly, conversational tone.

4. Action is specified clearly and logically.

5. A nice relevant close helps to create rapport and build bonds.

6. I don't see why we need 'Regards'. Just relevant contact details.

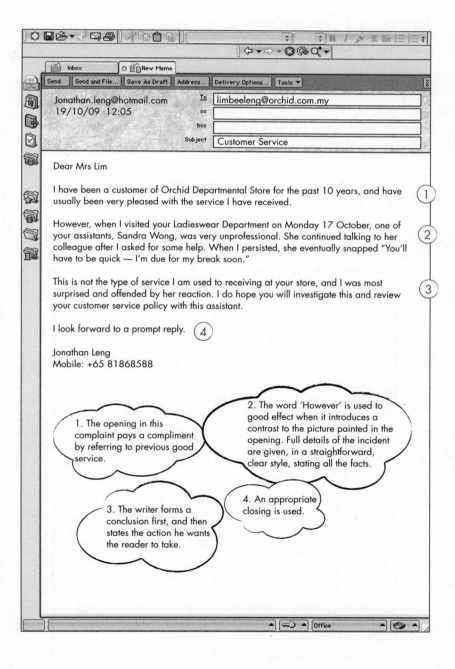

Jonathan.leng@hotmail.com   **To** limbeeleng@orchid.com.my
19/10/09 12:05   **cc**
                              bcc
                              Subject Customer Service

Dear Mrs Lim

I have been a customer of Orchid Departmental Store for the past 10 years, and have usually been very pleased with the service I have received.

However, when I visited your Ladieswear Department on Monday 17 October, one of your assistants, Sandra Wong, was very unprofessional. She continued talking to her colleague after I asked for some help. When I persisted, she eventually snapped "You'll have to be quick — I'm due for my break soon."

This is not the type of service I am used to receiving at your store, and I was most surprised and offended by her reaction. I do hope you will investigate this and review your customer service policy with this assistant.

I look forward to a prompt reply.

Jonathan Leng
Mobile: +65 81868588

1. The opening in this complaint pays a compliment by referring to previous good service.

2. The word 'However' is used to good effect when it introduces a contrast to the picture painted in the opening. Full details of the incident are given, in a straightforward, clear style, stating all the facts.

3. The writer forms a conclusion first, and then states the action he wants the reader to take.

4. An appropriate closing is used.

Using lists and bullets

Lists can be very useful in our writing. Sometimes when I'm writing a message I stop myself and think, "Hang on, I've just written one point, and I know I have another one. It will be better to use numbers or bullets." Lists are great because they help you to:

- organise your thoughts and your points.
- focus your reader's attention on key points.
- condense detailed or complicated topics.
- simplify the skimming process for busy readers.
- enhance visual impact.

Make sure, however, that your list items are parallel in structure. In this example, every point in this list needs to follow "if you" in the lead sentence.

> *You can improve your business writing if you:*
>
> - *adopt a friendly, conversational writing style.*
> - *read your message out loud to check the tone.*
> - *keep to the point and stay focused.*
> - *organise your points carefully with my Four Point Plan.*
> - *use language that your reader will understand.*

Notice how each point begins with a verb. This is a very good technique to use especially when writing a list of procedures or instructions for people to follow. Here's another list of bullet points, this time written in a different style, but still remembering grammatical parallelism:

> *Job responsibilities include:*
>
> - *Reception duties*
> - *Co-ordination of travel arrangements*
> - *Liaison with Finance Department on travel claims*
> - *Maintenance of databases*
> - *Preparation of catalogues and presentation materials*
> - *General office duties*

Here are two more e-mail messages with notes about the structure:

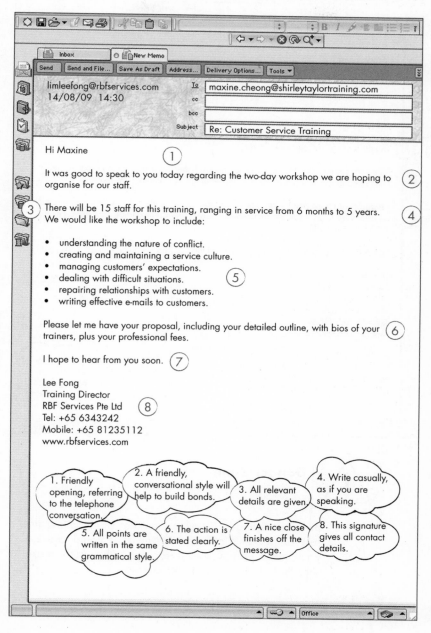

Hi Maxine ①

It was good to speak to you today regarding the two-day workshop we are hoping to organise for our staff. ②

③ There will be 15 staff for this training, ranging in service from 6 months to 5 years. We would like the workshop to include: ④

- understanding the nature of conflict.
- creating and maintaining a service culture.
- managing customers' expectations.
- dealing with difficult situations. ⑤
- repairing relationships with customers.
- writing effective e-mails to customers.

Please let me have your proposal, including your detailed outline, with bios of your trainers, plus your professional fees. ⑥

I hope to hear from you soon. ⑦

Lee Fong
Training Director
RBF Services Pte Ltd ⑧
Tel: +65 6343242
Mobile: +65 81235112
www.rbfservices.com

1. Friendly opening, referring to the telephone conversation.

2. A friendly, conversational style will help to build bonds.

3. All relevant details are given.

4. Write casually, as if you are speaking.

5. All points are written in the same grammatical style.

6. The action is stated clearly.

7. A nice close finishes off the message.

8. This signature gives all contact details.

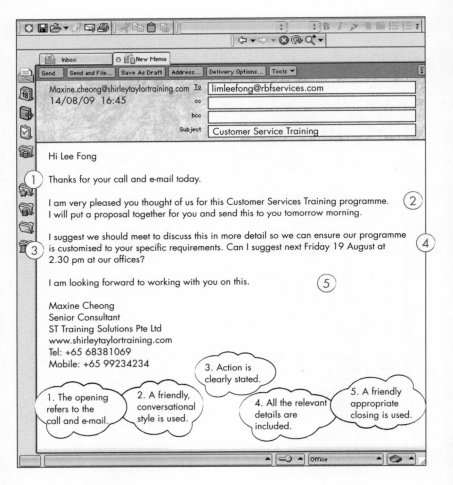

Hi Lee Fong

Thanks for your call and e-mail today.

I am very pleased you thought of us for this Customer Services Training programme. I will put a proposal together for you and send this to you tomorrow morning.

I suggest we should meet to discuss this in more detail so we can ensure our programme is customised to your specific requirements. Can I suggest next Friday 19 August at 2.30 pm at our offices?

I am looking forward to working with you on this.

Maxine Cheong
Senior Consultant
ST Training Solutions Pte Ltd
www.shirleytaylortraining.com
Tel: +65 68381069
Mobile: +65 99234234

1. The opening refers to the call and e-mail.

2. A friendly, conversational style is used.

3. Action is clearly stated.

4. All the relevant details are included.

5. A friendly appropriate closing is used.

 Danger Zone

Beware writing a list of points that don't follow the rule of grammatical parallelism as it could confuse your reader. If you start one point with a verb, make sure that all points start with a verb.

Star Tips for planning and structuring messages

1. Before beginning any message, ask yourself what's the purpose and what you want to achieve.

2. Remember to go through the seven-step process, and don't just hit 'Send' after your first attempt.

3. Use the Four Point Plan consistently to help you structure your messages logically.

4. Begin your message using your own words instead of those of our great-grandfathers.

5. Use a friendly conversational style instead of wooden, unnatural phrases.

6. Help the reader by including an action statement telling them exactly what you expect them to do.

7. Remember grammatical parallelism when compiling lists.

8. Make sure your message looks visually attractive.

9. Read your messages out loud so you can check if you are writing in a natural style.

CREATING BONDS AND DEVELOPING RAPPORT

7

"Revolve your world around the customer and more customers will revolve around you."

Heather Williams

Not so long ago it was primarily letters, meetings, face-to-face discussions and telephone conversations that had a huge bearing on our relationships with customers and colleagues. Today no one can deny the Internet era and the impact e-mail is having on our everyday business life. E-mail is now overtaking all the traditional methods and is becoming the chosen method of communication.

However, as we have already seen, with e-mail we can't see the writer, so we can't read any clues that may help us to interpret the message, e.g. tone of voice, gestures, body language. Therefore, e-mail holds a great potential for misunderstanding and misinterpretation — as many of us have already found out when e-mail sent or received has an unintended impact.

In this chapter we will be looking more specifically at tips and techniques that you can use to make your e-mail effective so that it works for you rather than against you. More specifically, because one of the main uses of e-mail is to keep in touch with customers, answer any queries, and resolve any problems, this chapter begins with a look at the general principles of good customer care.

Whether you are a home-based entrepreneur or a corporate tycoon, this chapter will show you how to use e-mail to enhance your relationships with your customers and co-workers.

 Fast Fact

Building relationships, whether online or offline, involves constant contact throughout the buying process. If you are to develop successful relationships, you need to learn about the buyer's wants and needs at each step, and then personalise each message so that it reflects the relationship you're building with that individual.

Seven deadly sins of online communication

Read this list of seven deadly sins of online communication and tick the ones that apply to you. If you tick a few of these items, you need help. This chapter will give you lots of advice on how to develop great relationships online.

1. You think what you say is more important than how you say it. ☐

2. You don't think it's important to present an e-mail message attractively with full sentences and a space between paragraphs. ☐

3. You don't know what is meant by creating a special bond with all customers, whether internal or external. ☐

4. You don't realise that a positive working attitude will prove an enjoyable and satisfying way to work. ☐

5. You think big customers should receive better attention than smaller ones. ☐

6. You get straight to the point in e-mail messages without including any emotions or feelings. ☐

7. You don't always answer your e-mail promptly. ☐

Using e-mail to build relationships

Customer care has been through many changes in the last few years. More and more companies are realising that positive action is needed to make customer satisfaction their prime aim. If companies are to fight the competitive battle, it is essential to make sure that the quality of their products or services is not just satisfactory, but exceptional.

Customers' expectations have changed a lot in recent years as well. Not only is there increased competition because of product similarity, customers are also much better informed and more willing to pay for value. Add to this the rising demand for improved support and the 'I want everything yesterday' mentality, and it's not difficult to see why attention to customer care is vitally important. Let's look at the perceptions of customer service in the past and how things look today.

Yesterday people wanted:	Today people want:
Best price	Best value
Satisfaction	Expectations to be exceeded
To get the job done	To get the job done promptly
Competence	A real bond, real connections

Fast Fact

If you don't take care of your customers, someone else will!

Creating a real bond

Everyone today is in the business of providing customer service. If you don't pay good attention to customer care skills in everything you do (and everything you do involves e-mail) you can be sure your customers will take their business somewhere else.

Studies show that it takes just 15 seconds for your customer to judge you when you first meet and greet him or her. During these 15 seconds your customer will decide if they will listen to you, believe you and trust you. More important, these 15 seconds will determine if they will buy from you!

The first impression a customer receives is influenced by three things — your words, your body language and your tone of voice. This pie chart shows clearly that it is your body language that is most important — it's *how* we say things that people pay more attention to.

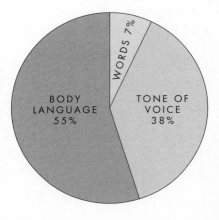

But, I hear you say, in e-mail you don't have the benefit of body language. True. All you have are words and tone, so you have to learn how to use these two aspects to create your own e-mail body language. When you learn to do this, you will be making a real connection — and that's what good customer care is all about.

 Aha! Moment

It's not *what* I say that's most important.
It's *how* I say it.

Compare these two e-mail messages and decide which one you think is going to help give a better impression and create a real bond.

1. Subject: Re: Problem solved

    Dear John — We spoke this morning, and glad to note your problem is solved. If you require any further assistance please revert.

    Thanks & Regards
    Mary Tan

2. Subject: Re: Problem solved

    Hi John

    Thanks for your call today.

    I'm so pleased that we've been able to find a solution to this. Good luck with future progress on this project.

    I'll be here when you decide how we can help you again.

    Mary

Danger Zone

So many people have a normal conversation with someone on the phone, and then write an e-mail in a stilted, formal way using words they would never use in speaking. E-mail should be used to help you build relationships, not break them. So don't undo all your good work on the phone by e-mailing in a different or unnatural style.

Aha! Moment

I should try to make sure that readers can hear my voice in an e-mail!

Myth Buster

When writing to someone for the first time, I should use very formal language.

On the contrary. Since you are not meeting face-to-face, you cannot offer a hearty handshake, a warm smile of welcome, or show your intense interest with your eyes or posture. While it is not easy, you must try very hard to get something of this in every message you send, particularly when writing to someone new.

Tips for building great relationships

Your aim must be to create an important connection with all your business contacts — a special bond. This applies whether you are dealing with a person face-to-face, over the telephone, in business meetings or through e-mail.

You can develop great relationships and bonds if you remember these tips:

- **Use the customer's name.** Everyone likes to hear their name, so use it. Begin your messages with a greeting and finish off with your name.

- **Avoid jargon.** If you must use words that the customer may not understand, be ready to explain.

- **Be friendly.** You don't want to come across as apathetic or indifferent. Smile and show warmth — it will make a difference.

- **Be confident and competent.** You must come over as knowledgeable instead of hesitant to unsure. Don't beat about the bush in your e-mail. Be clear and courteous.

- **Show empathy.** This is not the same as sympathy. You must show that you appreciate the other person's point of view or their problems, and a clear understanding of their feelings.

Aha! Moment

Yes, I can put a smile in my e-mail too!

Why should you try to do all this when you can get your job done just the same if you just go through the motions? Well, if you try to give a little extra in your day-to-day work, your contacts will feel better and you will feel better too. These principles are not only good for business, but they prove an enjoyable and satisfying way to work.

Fast Fact

It is easy to get a customer once. The challenge is keeping the customer. You can keep customers by creating partnerships, by creating bonds. Effective business writing will help.

Myth Buster

I should give my bigger customers better treatment than my not-so-big ones.

Who knows who will become your best customer tomorrow? The one you don't give a lot of attention today may well be the one who was planning to spend a lot of money with you tomorrow.

Let your readers sense your smile

Putting into practice the principles of good customer care is easier in person than over the telephone or through e-mail because you're dealing with a real person you can see and hear. It is easier over the telephone than through e-mail because even without seeing the person you can hear them and the tone of voice used — and yes, you can hear a smile in a voice. On e-mail you don't have either of these advantages, so you have to take other steps to try to let your readers sense your smile. Some techniques you can use are:

1. Lead your reader into the message

Try not to just dive into a message blindly. Ease the reader into the message by backtracking or giving some basic background information. Be warm and friendly where appropriate. For example:

> *Thanks for lunch last week. It was great to learn more about your new project, which sounds very interesting.*
>
> *I am glad we were able to speak on the telephone this morning. It was good to clarify this issue.*
>
> *Thanks for calling me today. It made a nice change to speak to a real person for a change instead of always dealing through e-mail!*
>
> *Your news today is interesting — it sounds like you've been working really hard to ensure the success of this project.*

2. Show some emotion

Some people give the mere facts and only the facts. They are so keen to get straight to the point that they forget to include any emotions, any feelings. Try to remember that emotive and sensory words add texture and dimension to the general message of what is being written.

You owe it to customers and colleagues to show empathy through your e-mail, using language that will help you in forming a better bond. For example:

I'll be pleased to help you sort out this problem.

I appreciate your understanding in trying to resolve this issue.

I hope I can shed some light on this very soon.

I see what you mean and can appreciate your concern.

This has given me a clearer perspective, and I can see a true picture now.

I'm happy to offer you an extra discount of 5% in the circumstances.

Danger Zone

Don't add so much emotion that you come over as too gushy. You only need a few extra words to really add something to your message and show some warmth.

3.   Use visual language

Try to paint a picture of what you are communicating. The reader will then be able to see the image that you are trying to create. Use phrases like:

I can see what you mean.

This is all very clear to me now.

This will now enable us to focus on our mutual goals.

Your suggestions look good.

I would like to take a look at this issue from another perspective.

Why should you care what people think?

I'm often told that some people don't care what others think of them based on their e-mails. They feel that it's not important, as long as the message gets across. Really? Do you really not care if you give a poor impression?

Think about it. In the morning when you get up, ask yourself why you take a shower, put on your nicely pressed clothes, fix your hair and make-up? Are you doing this because of what others may think of you if you don't? Not necessarily, right? You're doing it because you care about how you look.

When you write an e-mail in capital letters, filled with abbreviations, typos and grammatical errors, what do you expect the reader to think? When you forward e-mails with no comment and no thought as to what the recipient may think, how does that make you look? Believe me, people who don't know you will form an immediate impression about your standards and the sort of person you are — and it won't be a good one! They will wonder why you don't seem to care about how others view you. Those who know you well will probably shrug their shoulders and wonder why you can't be bothered to make a simple effort to show some courtesy and make a difference.

 Fast Fact

Perception is the only reality in e-mail. It's your choice whether you want to be perceived as educated and courteous. If you simply don't care, then that will be obvious too!

Remember, impressions are important, and you can control what they will be. All you have to do is understand the basic rules of e-mail etiquette and make a tiny bit of effort to display courtesy, consideration and common sense. It won't hurt, and believe me, the benefits are many.

If you are attending a meeting or visiting a client, you would make sure you are suitably dressed. When choosing the packaging for your new product, you always make sure it looks attractive and appealing. Similarly, you must present yourself appropriately online too. Does your e-mail look good? Have you checked to make sure there are no spelling errors? What's the first impression a new customer will receive from your e-mail message?

Myth Buster

It's only e-mail. Surely it doesn't matter what it sounds like, if I've made a spelling error, or even if it doesn't read quite right.

Wrong. If you don't feel that the spelling, the sound and the look of your e-mail are important, then you are saying that how you present yourself to customers and colleagues is also not important. The opposite is true. How your messages come across to other people has a great impact on readers' perceptions of you, as well as reflecting your communication skills and your professionalism.

Keeping it courteous while keeping it brief

Many people ask for advice about how to keep their messages short and to the point without coming across as being abrupt and cold. Well courtesy is important, of course, and it can be achieved with care and thought. Let's take a look at a few examples of how some messages could be improved while retaining clarity. Notice how all the improved versions are so much more personal and warm too:

☒ *Please find below the best available rate at The Westin Sydney.*
☑ *Here are our best available rates at The Westin Sydney.*

☒ *Kindly see attached on my department's performance for last month.*
☑ *Here is my performance report for March 2009.*

☒ *Your immediate feedback will be highly appreciated so we can advise the guest accordingly.*
☑ *Please let me have your urgent feedback so we can let the guest know.*

☒ With regards your enquiry on the distance from the Langkawi Orchid Hotel to the Langkawi Golf & Spa Resort. It is very close, around 5 minutes by taxi.

☑ Many thanks for your call. The Langkawi Orchid Hotel is just five minutes away from the Langkawi Golf & Spa Resort by taxi.

☒ Appreciate if you could provide us with the above information together with a contact number to reach you.

☑ Please let me have this information soon, together with your contact number.

☒ As per our telephone conversation, kindly find attached a copy of the credit card authorisation form.

☑ Thank you for your call. Attached is a copy of our credit card authorisation form.

☒ Please revert with your agreement to enable us to adjust the points on your account accordingly.

☑ We will be happy to adjust the points as soon as we receive your agreement.

☒ Kindly revert back with flight schedule upon confirmation and also with names of delegates, and liaise accordingly with our Martin Lim upon arrival at airport for transportation and hotel arrangements.

☑ Please let me know the delegates' names and their flight schedule. They should liaise with Martin Lim when they arrive regarding hotel arrangements.

☒ As spoken earlier with regards to your quotation ref xxxxx, pls advise whether possible for your goodself to come down to our company on 11 June (Wed) at 9.30 am for a short discussion with my senior technical manager on this issue.

☑ Thanks for your call today. It would be helpful if you could attend a short meeting with my senior technical manager. Is 9.30 am on Wednesday 11 June good for you?

☒ *Anticipating your soonest reply.*
☑ *Hope to hear from you soon.*
☑ *I look forward to your reply.*

Fast Fact

'Revert' does not mean 'reply'. It means to relapse or regress, to go back to a former condition. So please don't write, "*Please revert to me.*"

E-mail can affect careers

I was speaking to a Human Resource colleague recently and she told me that some of her staff are often rude and impulsive in their e-mails. They prefer to "shoot out e-mail" rather than discuss things face-to-face. This may not only affect workplace relationships, but it can also affect careers. Some employees seem to think they can vent their anger on the spot by hitting the 'Send' key, and this can easily erupt into an e-mail war. What we must remember is that e-mail sent out in haste can come back to haunt you. Apart from the possibility of landing you in court, it lowers productivity, and will almost never get the desired results. It's also not good for morale and job satisfaction.

Try This

Take a look at some of the e-mails you have sent recently. Consider how they could be improved to help you build better bonds with your readers.

Star Tips for creating bonds and developing rapport

1. Remember that how you say something is much more important than what you actually say.

2. Display your messages attractively, using full sentences and with a space between paragraphs.

3. Aim to create a special bond with all your customers — both external and internal.

4. Give smaller customers just as much attention as bigger ones.

5. Include feelings and emotions in your messages to add a more personal touch.

6. Answer all your e-mail promptly.

7. Remember that today's customers want solutions, not problems.

8. Use names in e-mail; be warm, friendly, empathetic — and remember to smile.

9. Use e-mail as a tool to enhance communication rather than as a replacement for communication.

NURTURING YOUR E-MAIL NETIQUETTE

"Manners are a sensitive awareness of the feelings of others. If you have that awareness, you have good manners, no matter what fork you use."

Emily Post

Etiquette refers to rules of good manners and behaviour, so 'netiquette' has become a set of rules for behaving appropriately online — network etiquette.

Cyberspace has its own culture, and whenever we enter a new culture it's bound to happen that we commit a few blunders. You may be misunderstood. You may offend people. You may take offence where none was intended. In cyberspace it's also easy to forget that you are interacting with real live human beings.

For all these reasons, many people make all kinds of mistakes.

Throughout this book we have talked about how to use e-mail effectively, how to write effective messages, how to use modern business language instead of yesterday's jargon, how to enhance your online communication, how to avoid the many pitfalls of e-mail, and so much more.

In this chapter, I hope to clear up some other key rules of the road for netiquette, and offer some general guidelines for behaviour in cyberspace. We will also look at some further aspects of e-mail, which may help make e-mail work individually for each reader. You may be superb at spelling, perfect at punctuation and great at grammar, in which case you may not need the guidelines mentioned here. However, some readers may be glad of an opportunity to brush up their cyber-grammar skills, so some readers may find it useful to recap by dipping in and out of this chapter.

I have also included some 'just for fun' items — emoticons and abbreviations. They should not really be used in business e-mail, but I have included them here for those of you who want to use them in personal messages.

Seven deadly sins of e-mail netiquette	
Read this list of seven deadly sins of e-mail netiquette and tick the ones that apply to you. If you tick a few of these items, you'll need to read this chapter carefully.	
1. You often send abb msgs to pple u know well. LOL.	☐
2. You write your e-mail messages sloppily because you don't consider it important for an e-mail message to be as perfect as a business letter.	☐
3. You don't run 'spell check' before you send a message, even though it's full of spelling errors.	☐
4. Your e-mail is often misunderstood because you never bother with your grammar and you often use the wrong words.	☐
5. You include emoticons in all your messages, whether personal or business. :)	☐
6. You never include an opening greeting or a closing in your e-mail messages.	☐
7. You often let your emotions get the better of you by writing angry or rude messages that upset your readers.	☐

Spruce up your cyber-grammar skills

Whether we like to admit it or not, we often judge people on first impressions, and vice versa. People look at the colour of our skin, our eyes, hair, our clothes, our age, even our weight. With e-mail this is not possible — but you will be judged by the quality of your writing. Spelling and grammar do count! So if you spend a lot of time on e-mail (and who doesn't?) it's worth brushing up on them.

I hope I will be forgiven by those of you who are fully conversant with the rules of good writing, punctuation and grammar. This may not be a section that you will need to refer to often. However, many people are unsure of precisely where an apostrophe should go, when to use a full stop instead of a comma, how to put together a grammatically correct sentence, and so on. This section should help you by clarifying all the fundamentals of the English language, punctuation and grammar.

Fast Fact

E-mail is a great informal method of communication, but that shouldn't be an excuse for carelessness or slopping writing. Use grammatically correct sentences and don't forget to do a spell check!

Perfect your punctuation

When you speak, the listener is helped by the intonation in your voice, pauses, emphasis, as well as body language. When you write, punctuation carries out all the same functions. Punctuation helps the reader to make sense of your writing.

Sentences are complete thoughts

Full stops, question marks and exclamation marks are used to mark the end of a sentence. A sentence contains a subject and a verb, and expresses a complete thought.

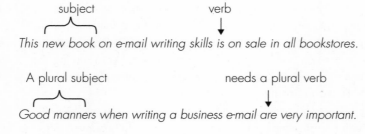

subject   verb

This new book on e-mail writing skills is on sale in all bookstores.

A plural subject   needs a plural verb

Good manners when writing a business e-mail are very important.

Fast Fact

You will avoid subject-verb agreement errors if you keep your sentences short and simple.

Very often people put commas where there should be full stops, as shown here:

☒ *It was good to see you last week, thanks for the great lunch.*
☑ *It was good to see you last week. Thanks for the great lunch.*

These are both complete thoughts.

☒ *I shall be in Seoul next month, however, my schedule is quite tight.*
☑ *I shall be in Seoul next month. However, my schedule is quite tight.*

These are both complete thoughts.

Fast Fact

'However' can be written in the middle of sentences or at the beginning, but do get the punctuation right. The use of 'however' is shown correctly in both these examples:

I am looking forward to going to China again next week. This time, however, I shall be speaking at a conference.

or

I am looking forward to going to China again next week. However, this time I shall be speaking at a conference.

Commas

Commas provide pauses in sentences, and they help to manage the flow of thought. Commas are used:

- when three or more items are listed:

    To connect to the Internet you will need a telephone line, a modem, a computer and an Internet service provider.

- to show where there would be a short natural pause if you were speaking:

  > *I believe this candidate has the relevant qualifications, but the other one has more experience.*

- to show where something has been added, like names, designations or other explanatory details:

  > *I will ask our Customer Service Manager, Robert Chan, to call you.*

  > *Fauziah Suki, my assistant, will speak to you soon about this.*

  > *Please switch off all electronic devices, including mobile phones, during the flight.*

Colons

Colons are used:

- to introduce a list:

  > *Many items are on sale today: telephones, computers, printers, fax machines.*

- to separate two clearly related ideas:

  > *My website gives more details of my books and seminars: www.shirleytaylor.com*

Semi-colons

Semi-colons are most commonly used to represent a pause longer than a comma and shorter than a full stop. However, it is possible to write perfect English without any semi-colons. Here are some examples of their use:

> *We must buy the new book for all staff; it will be useful for reference.*

> *These questions don't require answers; they are just intended to make you think.*

Apostrophes

Apostrophes seem to cause the most confusion, but they really aren't as difficult as they may seem. An apostrophe is used:

- to indicate omission of a letter or letters:

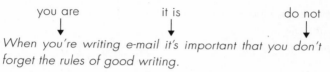

you are   it is   do not

When you're writing e-mail it's important that you don't forget the rules of good writing.

- to show ownership or possession:

Singular	Plural
the customer's problem	the customers' problems
the woman's shoes	the women's shoes
the director's car	the directors' cars
the manager's chair	the managers' chairs

Fast Fact

Remember that *it's* should only be used when you mean 'it is' or 'it has'.

It's been a lot of fun watching the puppy chasing its tail.

↑   ↑

It has   Don't use the apostrophe here

Practise your positivity

You can often improve the tone of your messages by adopting a positive attitude. Positive writing will give the reader a better impression, and will ultimately achieve better results. Read these negative sentences carefully and then study how they can be written more positively.

☒ *Have your report on my desk by 8 am tomorrow at the latest.*
☑ *Please let me have your report by 8 am tomorrow morning.*

☒ *You neglected to report these serious errors early enough.*
☑ *It is unfortunate that you did not report these errors earlier.*

☒ *I have looked through your report and am totally confused. Please see me urgently to clarify.*
☑ *I have several questions about your report. Let's meet soon to discuss this.*

☒ *This model is very popular but it only does 35 miles to the litre.*
☑ *This model is very popular and it does about 35 miles to the litre.*

☒ *If you do not return your form before 1 August you will be too late to attend the conference.*
☑ *Please return your form by 31 July so that we can register your name for the conference.*

☒ *I regret to inform you that the alterations will not be finished until next week.*
☑ *The alterations will be finished next Friday.*

Fast Fact

Negative language triggers negative results. Use positive words like these in your writing: results, guarantee, benefit, preferred, recommended, time-saving, safe, fast, proven, can, will.

Use active not passive voice

Passive voice is vague and puts a distance between you and your reader. It makes your sentences much longer, and it doesn't show any responsibility. Using active voice can considerably improve your writing style. Using active voice will:

- make the tone much more interesting and lively
- sound more personal and natural
- put people back into your writing
- show ownership and responsibility
- make your writing clear, specific and focused
- make your writing shorter

Here are some examples of changing passive to active voice:

☒ *Your order was received by us today.*
☑ *Thank you for your order, which we received today.*

☒ *The seminar was conducted by Robert Sim.*
☑ *Robert Sim conducted the seminar.*

☒ *Sales of X101 have exceeded all expectations.*
☑ *X101 sales have gone through the roof!*

☒ *A cheque should be obtained from your client.*
☑ *Please ask your client for a cheque.*

☒ *The monthly results were not included in your report.*
☑ *You did not include the monthly results in your report.*

☒ *You are requested to bring your own laptop to the workshop.*
☑ *Please bring your own laptop to the workshop.*

☒ *The signed employment contract should be returned by 14 April 2009.*
☑ *Please return the signed employment contract by 14 April 2009.*

☒ *Mobile phones are required to be switched off inside the salon.*
☑ *Please switch off mobile phones inside the salon.*

Try This

Be on the look out for passive sentences when you are reading other people's messages. Becoming aware in this way will help you to be more careful in using active voice in your own writing.

Electronic emotions

Although e-mail is generally thought of as informal, it is unfortunately devoid of the non-verbal communication that is so often taken for granted in real conversations. Facial expressions, body language and voice inflections are often used in speech to convey a lot of our meaning. For example, consider how you might interpret the meanings of this statement as the speaking emphasis varies in each case:

> *YOU told him that?*
> *You TOLD him that?*
> *You told HIM that?*
> *You told him THAT?*

In personal e-mail messages we can overcome the loss of this non-verbal expression by conveying emotions using emoticons. Another name for emoticons is 'smileys'.

To read these emoticons, tilt your head to the left:

Emoticon	Meaning
:-)	smiling
:-] or :-}	sarcastic smile
:'-(	crying
:-/	puzzled or confused
8-O	amazed
:-&	tongue-tied
:-O	yelling or screaming; or completely shocked
:-P	sticking out your tongue
:-I	can't decide how to feel; no feelings either way
;-)	winking
:-D	big delighted grin
:-[	fed up
:-()	can't (or won't) stop talking
:-X or :-#	my lips are sealed

Emoticons were developed in the early days of chat rooms, forums and newsgroups as users battled with the difficulties of typing in the way we talk. Emoticons evolved out of a need to bring subtle inflections and tones into written communication. For example:

> *Our staff retreat next month will be held in Bali! Isn't that great news? ;-)*

Abbreviations

In personal e-mail or in chat rooms, abbreviations are often used. These help people to cut down on typing. So many new abbreviations are being thought up all the time, and it's often quite difficult to keep pace with them all. I also feel they can be over-used and sometimes taken to extremes. However, I'm including a list of the most commonly used abbreviations in case you want to join 'the club'.

Abbreviation	Meaning
b4	before
BFN	bye for now
BCNU	be seeing you
BTW	by the way
CUL	see you later
F2F	face-to-face
FWIW	for what it's worth
IMHO	in my humble opinion
IOW	in other words
ITRW	in the real world
JIC	just in case
L8R	later
LOL	laughing out loud
OTF	on the floor (laughing)
TIA	thanks in advance
TPTB	the powers that be
TTYL	talk to you later
TOL	tons of love
TTFN	ta ta for now
<g> or <G>	grin
<bg>	big grin

Danger Zone

Remember to use such abbreviations only when you are sure the recipient will understand them. And if you write to me, please don't use them at all!

Myth Buster

It's OK to use emoticons and abbreviations in business e-mail messages. It helps to lighten things up, right?

My feeling is that it's rarely appropriate to use emoticons and abbreviations in business e-mail. If you express yourself clearly in words and full sentences your personality will shine through!

Netiquette — A summary

In personal relationships we have etiquette. In e-mail we have netiquette. This is something I have discussed a lot throughout this book. In this section I will give you my own personal definition of netiquette.

Etiquette is defined in the Concise Oxford Dictionary as 'conventional rules of personal behaviour in polite society'. I would define netiquette as 'a set of rules for acceptable behaviour on e-mail that have evolved from experience'. Always observe these guidelines:

Never ever leave a response too long. It is common courtesy to respond to a message as quickly as you can — even if you have to say that a detailed response will be sent later.

E-mail addresses must be correct. Correctly addressed e-mail messages are received within seconds, but it can take a while to receive an error message letting you know that an incorrectly addressed message wasn't delivered.

Take off the caps lock. DON'T SHOUT! Even if you want to get noticed please do not use capitals in e-mail messages. It is like shouting, it is considered rude and will usually be counter-productive. And also…NEVER RESORT TO EXCESSIVE PUNCTUATION*@!!**?!!!!

Informality is OK in e-mail. Replace formal salutations like 'Dear David' with 'Hi David' or even just 'David'. Similarly, replace 'Yours sincerely' with 'See you soon' or some other informal closing.

Question your subject headings. People are most likely to read important-looking e-mails first. Give your messages a clear and specific (SMART) subject heading.

Use short sentences and short paragraphs. The shorter your messages, the more likely they will be read and understood. Remember to paragraph just as you would in other business documents.

Enumerate with numbers or bullets. Present your messages attractively. Use numbers, bullets or sub-headings if possible — this will add to the clarity of your messages.

Tidy up long sentences to eliminate waffle. Tapping away at the keyboard as you think can sometimes cause your sentences to become too long. Read through your messages carefully to improve clarity and understanding.

Take pride in your finished message. Make sure your message is accurate, brief and clear as well as attractively presented and logically structured. In this way it will be understood and will achieve the desired results.

Ensure everything is right before you hit 'Send'. You cannot call a message back for second thoughts, so get it right the first time!

Aha! Moment

E-mail reflects my personality and creates an impression of me. I'd better make sure it's a good one.

Last word on netiquette

Do you run the risk of causing yourself a great deal of damage through using e-mail in an inappropriate way, or taking your e-mail for granted? It's true that we are now sending more e-mail messages than ever before. We even e-mail people sitting at the next cubicle instead of walking a few steps. (Go on, admit it!) The problem is, this familiarity and convenience is encouraging us to nurture sloppy, dangerous habits — habits that can ruin our reputations!

Let's look at some facts:

- Careless e-mail, especially if you slander someone, could land you in court.
- E-mail is never completely private. Something you wrote could come back to haunt you. Your message may also be posted on your company's notice board, or mailed to a competitor.
- E-mail messages can be used in legal investigations or as evidence in lawsuits.
- E-mail passwords can be stolen.
- E-mail messages are monitored by your IT department. Violating company policies may cost you your job.
- Careless and sloppy e-mailing can tarnish your reputation.

So before you hit 'Send' again, ask yourself the following questions:

- Could I say this to the person's face?
- Am I violating any policies or laws?
- Would I want this message forwarded to someone else?
- Is the information in a logical order and easy to read?
- Am I writing this while I'm angry or upset?
- Will the reader know clearly what to do in response?
- Will my e-mail give a good impression of me?
- Is e-mail the best way to deliver this information?
- Is e-mail more appropriate than phone or face-to-face communication?
- Will my e-mail get the right results?

If your answers are 'yes', you can now hit 'Send'!

Star Tips for nurturing your e-mail netiquette

1. Use emoticons and abbreviations only in personal e-mail, not business e-mail.

2. Spruce up your cyber-grammar skills and make sure your punctuation, grammar, spelling and business language are first-class.

3. Write in a simple, relaxed and straightforward style and an appropriate tone.

4. Take pride in your finished message. It should be logically structured and attractively presented if it is to be understood and achieve results.

5. Get your message right first time. Once you hit 'Send' it could be in the recipient's inbox and be read within seconds.

6. Use positive words to create a positive impression.

7. Active voice is much better than passive voice, which will date your writing.

8. Take care that your messages are not rude, offensive or slanderous.

9. Don't engage in unethical behaviour on the Internet.

10. Keep up-to-date with new developments and new technology so that you can make the most of their full potential.

PRACTISING SAFE E-MAIL

"Every solution breeds new problems."

Murphy's Law

9

Just as in the real world there are people who commit shameful acts of misbehaviour, so it is also true in the world of cyberspace. While these people are in the minority, we still have to be aware and be on the lookout for them. This chapter will help to increase your awareness of the mischief and trouble that can be caused in the world of e-mail, and tells you how to spot it and stop it.

Seven deadly sins of e-mail abuse	
Read this list of seven deadly sins of e-mail abuse and tick the ones that apply to you. If you tick a few of them, you need help. This chapter will help you to practise safe e-mail.	
1. You think spam is a tin of chopped luncheon meat.	☐
2. You always send an abusive note back when you have been spammed.	☐
3. You send lots of unsolicited sales letters to potential clients 'just in case'.	☐
4. Your direct e-mail blasts are always several pages long.	☐
5. When you send a message to lots of people you include every e-mail address in the 'To' section.	☐
6. You always forward chain letters to the stipulated number of people just in case something awful happens.	☐
7. You spend hours finding jokes on the Internet and sending them to your friends because everyone loves jokes, don't they?	☐

Who goes there? Friend or foe?

Virtually everyone with an e-mail address will receive a certain amount of spam. Spamming is sending an unsolicited e-mail to people who have neither asked for it nor particularly want to receive it. It is the electronic equivalent of junk postal mail and direct-mail selling. Junk postal mail is considered by most people to be annoying and wasteful; junk e-mail is even more so.

At least with postal mail we can throw the envelope away without opening it. With junk e-mail you have to take time to read at least the first few lines before finding out that it's junk! This is not only time-wasting, it is also inconsiderate and very bad netiquette!

The first spam e-mail was sent on 3 May 1978. It was sent to people taken from a (then printed) directory of ARPANET users, mostly at universities and corporations. ARPANET was the first major wide-area computer network. When a company called DEC released a new computer and operating system with ARPANET support, one of their marketers felt the news should be shared with ARPANET users and administrators. So he looked up addresses, briefed his boss about potential complaints from the mass e-mail, and delivered it to about 60 recipients. Some found the message vaguely relevant, but in general it was not well received — and it was the last commercial mass e-mail for many years to come.

Unfortunately, this lesson was unlearned, and spam has become the plague of the Internet, with literally millions of unwanted e-mail messages being sent to mailboxes around the world every day, particularly those of an 'adult' nature. Spam is crippling the backbone of the Internet and causing frustration and anger to its recipients.

Fast Fact

Spam received its name from a famous sketch from the British comedy show, *Monty Python's Flying Circus*, in which a café had only the canned luncheon meat called 'Spam' on its menu. Even when a customer complained that he doesn't like Spam, the café staff made it quite clear that he could have anything he liked — but everything came with Spam!

Spam is easy enough to recognise. Here are a few examples:

> *Subject: Make lots of $$$$$$$ fast!*
> *Subject: DON'T MISS THIS BIG PRIZE GIVEAWAY*
> *Subject: Let us help you revamp your life?*
> *Subject: 108 Secrets to Achieve Prosperity — Revealed!*
> *Subject: New laptop for you FREE!!*

 Aha! Moment

If anything sounds too good to be true, it probably is!

Other spammers put in totally inappropriate subject lines to try to tempt you to read them, such as:

> *Subject: I enjoyed our meeting!*
> *Subject: It was a great date!*
> *Subject: Can we meet up soon?*

Spam covers everything from get rich quick schemes to weight loss miracles, even getting a diploma online, so remember — just hit 'Delete'!

Spam may not cost much for the originator, but there are additional costs that must be borne by others, as well as the frustration:

- The time each recipient spends reading the message.
- Computer processing time on each server.
- Storage time as the message waits on your ISP's server.
- Bandwidth consumption, which may slow access for others.
- Distress caused when the message is totally inappropriate for the audience.

Some angry recipients of spam try to take matters into their own hands by sending rude or abusive messages, known as 'flame' mail, to the originators, or by 'mail-bombing' them (sending huge files of useless information which clog up their mailboxes). Unfortunately, this only makes matters much worse by adding to the volume of useless information that is already clogging up the arteries of the Internet.

Scam spam or hopeful spam?

The first thing we need to do is become aware about what's 'scam spam' and what's 'hopeful spam'. We all receive lots of scam spam trying to get us to click on websites that will try to sell us something that will improve our lives in some way (I'm trying to be polite here!) This is the sort of scam spam that we must not reply to. This would just make matters much worse. You would never think twice about throwing paper junk mail in your trash bin without reading it, so don't think twice about deleting scam spam like this. I wouldn't even bother to click on the 'unsubscribe' button of such spam, because this type of underhanded spammer is well-known for using such removal requests as a means of validating e-mail addresses that are 'live' (in use). In this way you will find yourself getting more spam rather than less.

However, there's also hopeful spam. For example, I receive lots of e-mail telling me about conferences and seminars, which are legitimate events. This sort of message is not trying to involve me in anything illegal or underhanded, so after skimming it in case it contains anything interesting I will probably quickly hit 'Delete'. With this type of hopeful spam I would also not hesitate to use the unsubscribe button to remove myself from their mailing list without fearing any terrible repercussions.

Aha! Moment

I must become spam savvy by learning what constitutes scam spam and what's hopeful spam, and deal with both appropriately.

Here are some other steps you can take to help yourself as well as other innocent recipients of spam:

1. Use different e-mail addresses for business and personal use, or when surfing the Internet, so that you only risk getting spam at this e-mail address and reduce the spam coming to the e-mail address you use more often.

2. Report scam spam to the ISP (Internet Service Provider) whose services are used by spammers.

3. Use the filter facility for terms that you find offensive, so any such e-mails are delivered straight into your trash.

4. Don't include your e-mail address on every page of your website. Spammers have sophisticated software that collects any e-mail address it finds on websites.

5. Do not patronise any of the companies whose goods and services are promoted by spam.

6. Guard your e-mail address carefully and do not give permission to anyone else to share the details you give, for example, when filling in forms.

7. Unsubscribe to any services or newsletters that you don't wish to receive.

8. Do not give permission for your e-mail address to be passed on to other parties when you subscribe to or register for a new service. Be sure to tick or clear the relevant preference box.

Spam filters

If you use a corporate e-mail system, your organisation probably has a spam filter that makes sure you don't receive too much spam. In my mind, this is essential. I use a spam filter too, and according to the statistics at the time of writing, 44.68 per cent of my mail is spam. Of course, I still need to go into my 'Unverified' list at least once a day, just to authorise any legitimate senders who may be stuck there. But this is far less a hindrance to me than seeing all that *!*$*!!! in my inbox!

Flamers and trolls

A 'troll' is someone who posts offensive comments, derogatory statements or generally inflammatory messages in discussion groups or chat rooms. Trolls use language that we all know would lead to a fight if used in the local pub. Trolls have the intention of provoking others into an emotional response, and they generally just want to disrupt normal discussion.

A 'flame' is a nasty message or a personal attack on another e-mailer. People are often tempted to send an obnoxious message when they receive spam and chain letters. However, such replies also tie up the arteries of the Internet and should be avoided. Sometimes, flamers attempt to assert their authority or establish a position of superiority over other users. Other times, a flamer is simply an individual who believes he or she carries the only valid opinion. This leads him or her to personally attack anyone who disagrees. If you receive a flame you have several choices:

- Apologise if you annoyed the other person
- Respond with your own flame and start a war
- Ignore it

If you agree that it's not nice to flame and if you want to avoid flames, here is some advice:

- Never send unsolicited e-mail advertising your product or service. This is neither professional nor ethical, and you may be blacklisted.
- Never insult other people's culture, customs, religious beliefs or their country. All these topics are very sensitive, especially when talking to strangers. You may be using a machine to get the message across, but remember there is a human being at the other end, and human beings have feelings. Be very careful with sensitive topics.
- Avoid ambiguities. Make sure your message is crystal clear and appropriate so that it doesn't result in misunderstanding.
- Never correct a correspondent's grammar or spelling, unless you are specifically asked. The writer may take offence. If you are not sure what a message means you can ask for clarification — but do so tactfully. Remember the writer may not be writing in their native language.

Mail bombing

Mail bombing is when someone sends a huge amount of e-mail to one specific address with the sole intention of disrupting their service. Perhaps someone is angry at something you did or saw your comments in a discussion forum. This person may decide to take vengeance by flooding your mailbox. If you receive the same message 1,000 times, it may take up the space allocated for your mailbox or even cause your server to crash.

Companies who abuse e-mail by sending out unsolicited mail advertising their products or services are often the target of mail bombers.

Mail bombing is not only annoying, it is also illegal. Violators can be prosecuted. If you receive a mail bomb, report it to your service provider immediately. It's also a good idea to inform the sender's service provider about it.

Chain letters

I'm sure you must have received one of those letters promising you untold riches if you just send a dollar to a list of people. The same letter threatens you that horrible things will happen to you or your loved ones within a very short time if you don't follow the instructions. The people who begin such chains are mischief-makers. Unfortunately the same sort of thing happens on e-mail.

Chain e-mails often start with a pleasant little story about a happy event, or tell you about something positive and emotive. They then instruct you to send the message on to several more people, warning you that bad luck will befall you and your loved ones if you break the chain. Here's an extract from a chain letter:

Subject: Must read!

Dear Friends

You may have already seen this, but in case you haven't, read on … Read these spectacular thoughts on the new year. All it takes is a few seconds to read and think about them. Do not keep this message. This mantra must leave your hands within 48 hours. You will get a very pleasant surprise. This is true even if you are not superstitious.

Chain mail is written by people who get a kick out of wasting other people's time. They usually do it for fun or to cause trouble.

Chain mail has no place on the Internet. If you receive any chain letters, you can beat the chain mailers by not following the instructions and by refusing to be taken in by them. Forward a copy to your system administrator or postmaster and they may be able to put a stop to such messages.

Hoaxes

A progression from chain mail is hoax mail. These are messages asking you to do something or send something in support of a completely fictitious goal. Innocent new users often pass on these hoax messages to all their friends, and before long thousands of e-mail inboxes around the world are clogged with them. They waste money in connection costs, they waste time, they waste resources and they slow down systems.

One of the most famous hoaxes is called 'Little Craig'. Several years ago Craig was diagnosed with an inoperable brain tumour. Craig decided that before he died he wanted to get into the Guinness Book of Records for receiving the most get well cards. He achieved his ambition, and also thankfully made a full recovery. However, this turned into an e-mail hoax requesting people to send Craig business cards by snail mail. At the last count, Craig was still receiving bags full of business cards every day. If you receive this story in your inbox, please tell the person who sent it that it is a hoax, and delete it!

Have you ever seen the hoax about Bill Gates? It begins with something like this:

Subject: Free Microsoft products

My name is Bill Gates. Here at Microsoft we are working on a tracing program that will track everyone who receives this message.

The message proceeds to promise money and free Microsoft products if you are one of the lucky e-mailers who forward this message.

This is an elaborate hoax, which was not written by Bill Gates, so don't sit waiting for the cash to drop through your mailbox.

Fast Fact

There are several sites that cover hoaxes, scams and chain letters. Here are some:

Hoaxbusters: http://hoaxbusters.org

Symantec Virus Hoaxes: http://www.symantec.com/avcenter/hoax.html

Snooping

On some networks, it is often quite easy to obtain access to another person's electronic files. If you should be in a position where it is easy to do this, please resist the temptation. If you were visiting someone's home you wouldn't sneak upstairs and take a peek in their drawers, would you? If you were passing someone's house you wouldn't try the door and look inside if it was open. The same goes for e-mail — let's respect other people's privacy.

Harassment

We sometimes hear of cases of sexual harassment in the office, but now some people are taking this a step further by harassing their colleagues via e-mail. I have read of cases where male supervisors send business e-mail to female colleagues that start off businesslike and then continue with sexual innuendo or harassment. It may start off as something apparently innocent such as, 'Your hair looks good in this new style', but sometimes it has been known to progress to completely unacceptable levels.

If you are ever on the receiving end of any kind of e-mail harassment, be sure to keep copies noting the times and dates. If the situation becomes intolerable, you can take the evidence to your human resources department and they will deal with the culprit accordingly.

Danger Zone

Abusive language and disturbing behaviour is never a good idea, and on e-mail it is a definite no-no. If you don't want to see your words splashed on the cover of your local newspaper, then don't hit 'Send'.

Jokes and cartoons

Some jokes are funny. Some jokes quite simply are not. Others are far too long and we just haven't got time to read them. Receiving joke after joke in your inbox can become downright irritating. It beats me how so many seemingly busy people have the time to search the Web for these jokes in the first place — let alone spend time sending them out to unsuspecting recipients.

Downloading cartoons or funny attachments can also be quite irritating — for some people it may take 15 minutes to download an attachment, and then for what? For some cartoon that you thought was funny, but your friend may not. Before you send out jokes and cartoons to everyone in your address book ask yourself if the recipient will be pleased to receive them. Remember also that the person you e-mail may not appreciate your sense of humour. The golden rules are: be selective, and be cautious.

Star Tips for practising safe e-mail

1. Stay safe by being aware of what's scam spam and what's hopeful spam.

2. Never be rushed into responding to e-mail that may be spam.

3. Never send anyone any money through an e-mail request.

4. Never give out any personal information such as your password, telephone number or, worse still, your credit card details.

5. Never respond to spam and chain letters, and never forward them.

6. Never insult anyone's beliefs, culture, customs, religion or country.

7. Be wary of hoax messages and learn to identify them.

8. If you don't want to see your offensive words splashed on the cover of a magazine, do not hit 'Send'.

9. Remember, just because it is written doesn't necessarily mean it's true.

SAFETY AND SECURITY

"There are two types of encryption: one that will prevent your sister from reading your diary and one that will prevent your government."

Bruce Schneier

With e-mail becoming a universal means of communication, security and privacy are important. The area of security is developing rapidly. In this chapter we will look at some of the important security aspects that you must consider when using e-mail in your business.

Seven deadly sins of e-mail safety and security
Read this list of seven deadly sins of e-mail safety and security, and tick the ones that apply to you. If you tick a few of these items, you need to check out this chapter.
1. You think you're the only person who can read your e-mail messages. ☐
2. You have never changed your password. ☐
3. You think encryption is something out of the movie *Superman*. ☐
4. You frequently hit 'Send' before thinking carefully about the content of the message. ☐
5. You sometimes leave your desk while your mailer is still online and on-screen. ☐
6. Your company is always thinking of writing an e-mail policy but still hasn't got around to it. ☐
7. You always forward virus-related messages to everyone you know, 'just in case'. ☐

Is my e-mail secret?

E-mail often feels personal and intimate, so much so that it lulls you into a certain sense of privacy and/or a false sense of security. Well here's something you should know: e-mail is not secret. In a large organisation, several other people may have access to your e-mail messages. There is the system administrator who monitors the e-mail system in your company. Other workstations could also feasibly access your message while they are in transit over your network. Computer programs for monitoring message activity are often used. These monitoring programs can produce an abundance of information about e-mail messages sent and received in an organisation.

While you may question the ethical values of enabling mail to be read by many different parties, the bottom line is that your employer owns the system and therefore also the messages on the system. They aren't just plain nosey. Here are some reasons why it is desirable for your e-mail messages to be monitored:

- Employers may need to produce e-mail messages as evidence in a court of law.

- Employers may need evidence of activities that are detrimental to the business.

- Employers may be concerned about staff conducting inappropriate activities.

- Employers may be concerned about staff running business outside.

- Employers may need to access e-mail for staff who are on holiday, especially if anything unexpected happens.

- A wrongly addressed message could be returned undelivered, so the system administrator may see this. If you are e-mailing anything you shouldn't be, you could be found out.

- The recipient of your message may innocently (or otherwise) pass it on to someone else.

- Your company's e-mail messages could have a high value if they were to fall into the wrong hands. Hackers are clever but vicious thieves who can read your messages for malicious purposes.

Fast Fact

E-mail messages are much like postcards sent through the postal service. A postcard can be read by anyone who handles it, and may end up pinned on your office notice board. E-mail is very much an open medium, even with encryption. Remember this and treat all your e-mail messages as having a similar degree of openness as a postcard.

Why is security an issue?

One of the main problems with e-mail security is that an e-mail message usually travels through many different places before reaching its final destination. A message addressed to you may pass through about 10 Internet servers before it reaches your inbox. There are several points along the path of the e-mail where security could be compromised:

- A message could be tampered with before it leaves your company's server. Your system administrator has access to user names and passwords, and may have full access to read, alter, delete or create e-mail using any user's name.

- Your company's e-mail server or your ISP could be targeted by a hacker.

- E-mail messages can be tampered with on the server at their destination. In the same way that the sender's system administrator could potentially change a message, the same is true at the receiving end.

- Problems with authentication can make it difficult to confirm the identity of senders and recipients. Without security, you cannot be certain that you are actually corresponding with the person named on the e-mail.

Controlled access

Although there are legitimate reasons why people should be allowed to access your e-mail system, there are a few ways you can control such access:

User ID and password

These are used to control access to your e-mail system by users on a network or users with shared access. Remember the golden rules:

- Never tell anyone your password. A password needs to be easy to remember while at the same time being a little obscure. Some people prefer to use a short word followed by a series of numbers. Don't use anything obvious like your child's name, your nickname or your car registration number.

- Change your password frequently.
- Exit your e-mail when you have to leave your workstation for any length of time.
- Use a screen saver that is protected with another password.

Firewalls

A firewall is a system that acts at network level and is designed to protect an organisation's private network system from external intrusion via the Internet. The firewall allows only certain authorised messages in from and out to the Internet. Organisations that use firewalls will usually have a security policy that specifies who is responsible for configuring and managing the firewall, perhaps in the form of a central IT department. In practice, firewalls are used to check addresses and the type of incoming messages. They do not check the content of the messages — this is the role of filters and virus checkers.

Encryption

If your company's e-mail could in any way be damaging if it fell into the wrong hands, then the solution is to encrypt the information. Encryption is a security process that scrambles information so that it can only be unscrambled by someone with an appropriate decryption key. This can be a very effective system, as long as the key remains secret. Other people may be able to decode messages, but not without a vast amount of hard work and computer power.

The encryption software needed to encode your message could be placed in one of three areas:

- Within the client program. In this case, everything you send from your personal workstation will be encoded.
- On the company's mail server. In this case internal messages are not encoded, but any mail going outside the company will be encrypted.
- In the firewall, or security filter. In this case only mail that arrives through a firewall will be encrypted.

There are two main types of encryption:

Symmetric encryption

Here both the sender and the recipient share the same secret key. This key is used both to encrypt and decrypt messages. Symmetric encryption is relatively fast. It is used mainly in an organisation's internal network where the system administrator will issue the same key to all users.

Asymmetric encryption

Here each user has two keys: a public key that is freely available and is used to encrypt messages, and a private key that is known only to the recipient and is used to decrypt messages. When someone wants to send you a message, he or she needs to obtain your public key to encrypt the message before sending it to you. As you are the only person with the private key, you will be the only one able to read the message. If a message goes astray or is intercepted in transit by a system administrator, it appears as unreadable scrambled characters because you are the only person who has the key to read it. Asymmetric encryption is slower but it is more valuable when communicating with external organisations or through the Internet.

Your private key or code is part of your electronic identity. Do not give it to anyone or write it out somewhere that others can find it.

For a simpler method of encryption you could write your message in Word, save it with a password, compress it with something like WinZip, and then attach it to an e-mail message. This is a longer way of sending messages but it does make it difficult for snoopers to view them.

Digital signatures

A digital signature provides confirmation of the origin of an electronic document similar to the way a handwritten signature on a letter confirms that it was composed and signed by a certain person. However, a digital signature provides far more security. Using a digital signature makes it possible to verify that the person signing the message actually created it, verify the time the message was signed, and also verify that it has not been tampered with since it was signed. Public-key encryption similar to that used to encrypt messages is also used to implement digital signatures.

Digital signatures are automatically interpreted by the mailer, which will inform you if the message has been compromised in any way. If your mailer is not able to interpret digital signatures, you will still be able to read digitally signed messages — you will just not have the assurance provided by the digital signature.

Digital certificates

Another possible solution to the problem of e-mail security is provided by the process of certification, which takes digital signatures one step further. In this process, digital signatures are authenticated by a third party, who puts an electronic 'seal' around the message. These electronic certificates may be provided by your own company or alternatively they may be issued by an independent, trusted third party. This third party, known as a Certification Authority, confirms the identity of the person or organisation in whose name the certificate is issued.

The best known package that uses digital signatures, digital certificates and public/private keys is known as Pretty Good Privacy (PGP). This software integrates with your e-mail software and provides a wide range of powerful facilities for encryption.

When you receive encrypted messages, you can set up your e-mail system so that it automatically decrypts them using your private key. It is no different from reading ordinary e-mail messages.

In the past, digital signatures and encryption required both sender and recipient to have similar mailer and encryption software installed. However, MIME and Secure-MIME (or S-MIME) have been developed to allow different e-mail systems to communicate securely. This makes it easier for people using a variety of different mailers to exchange encrypted messages.

Encryption is a developing area in e-mail and it will most likely be used more widely in the future as S-MIME evolves.

 Fast Fact

The governments of some countries restrict the use of encryption technology because of concern about it being used to hide criminal activities.

Other techniques to protect your messages

Apart from using encryption and other technologies to ensure the security of your messages, there are several other steps you can take to protect yourself.

- **Protect your password.** Your password is the most vulnerable point in e-mail security. Guard it safely and change it regularly.

- **Never leave your desk while your mailer is still online.** Unscrupulous individuals could read your mail or send a message from your e-mail address.

- **Think twice before you hit 'Send'.** Even if you use encryption, it can still be passed on once the recipient has decrypted it. Think carefully about the content of all your messages and imagine them as open documents that could end up on the screen of the person you would least like to see them.

- **Know your company's e-mail policy.** If your company has a published policy with regard to e-mail, then read it carefully. Check also if it includes anything regarding personal use of e-mail. You must operate within company guidelines.

- **Respect other people's privacy if you expect them to respect yours.** Don't forward any e-mail messages if it could cause distress or embarrassment to the person who sent it originally; don't snoop into other people's mail; and don't read messages that someone else has printed out and not yet collected.

Computer viruses

The threat of computer viruses is very real. A virus may corrupt or delete data from your computer, use your e-mail program to spread the virus to other computers, or even erase everything on your hard disk.

The main worry of viruses comes from attachments. It is very dangerous to download e-mail attachments without taking proper precautions. Therefore when you receive a message with an attached file, do not download the attachment unless you know the sender and you are sure that what is being sent is legitimate, and also that you have anti-virus software installed on your machine.

Viruses can be disguised as attachments of funny images, greeting cards, or audio and video files. Viruses also spread through downloads from the Internet. They can be hidden in illicit software or other programs that you may download.

Once a virus is on your computer, its type or the method it used to get there is not as important as removing it and preventing further infection.

Macro viruses

These are the most prevalent type of virus around at the moment. A macro virus is a virus that's written using macro language — this means language built into a software application such as a word processor. Some applications (for example, parts of Microsoft Office) allow macro programs to be embedded in documents, so that the programs may run automatically when the document is opened. Therefore, this provides a clear mechanism by which viruses can spread.

Macro viruses are most likely to be found in offices because they are often passed along over networks and via e-mail attachments. According to some estimates, 75 per cent of all viruses today are macro viruses. Once a macro virus gets onto your computer, it can embed itself in all future documents you create.

 Fast Fact

In 1990 there were around 200 to 500 reported viruses. In 1991, estimates ranged from 600 to 1,000. In late 1992, the number went up to 2,300. By 1996 the number climbed over 10,000. In 2000 the number reached 50,000. It is easy to say there are probably well over 100,000 computer viruses now!

Anti-virus software

The best way to prevent viruses is to install anti-virus software on your computer. This usually checks any attachments automatically when you give the instruction to download them from your e-mail.

At network level it is also possible to install virus checkers that are configured to scan all incoming and outgoing messages for viruses. Any messages that are found to contain a suspected virus will be rejected or sent to a specified e-mail address where further investigation can be undertaken.

Hoax viruses

Does this sound familiar?

> 'Don't read or open any e-mail titled Good Times! It will destroy your computer.'

Most of us have received messages similar to this one, warning that your computer will face certain doom if you open such e-mail and read it. The truth is these warnings are a hoax. You can't get a virus or any system-damaging software by reading an e-mail message. E-mail messages themselves cannot contain viruses. Since e-mail is not a system file in that sense, viruses cannot exist there.

To find more information on specific hoax viruses, look up the many useful sites on the Internet. For example: www.vmyths.com, www.hoaxbusters. org, www.hoaxbusters.net, www.hoax-slayer.com.

We can all play a part in stopping these hoaxes from spreading by never forwarding any hoax messages. It will only exacerbate the problem. If you receive a copy of a hoax warning from a friend, simply reply to the person who sent it to you stating that it is a hoax. Don't be angry with the person because they probably forwarded the message to you in all innocence.

 Fast Fact

E-mail can be a double-edged sword. It can be an enormous benefit as the extremely efficient business tool that it is, but very dangerous if used inappropriately.

How can I protect my computer from real viruses?

Take these precautionary steps:

- Never download or run an attached file on an e-mail message from a stranger or from an unknown address. Be very cautious when downloading or running one from a friend as they can easily pass you a virus unwittingly.

- Never have your e-mail program set to run attached files automatically. This is especially true for browsers and/or e-mail programs that automatically execute Microsoft Word after opening an e-mail message. Turn off this option.

- Never run an executable file you've just received without first running it through an anti-virus program.

- If your computer is on a network, make sure you have security steps in place to prevent unauthorised users putting files on your computer. Networks are ideal virus transmitters since they are accessed by many computers and there is usually a great deal of interaction between them.

- Make sure you have a good anti-virus program that is updated constantly.

- Keep your e-mail software updated. Software companies are always finding problems with their products, and if they are good about it, they will post patches to update your e-mail software. Continually check your software company's website for security updates.

Star Tips for for e-mail safety and security

1. Remember, Big Brother is always watching. There are good reasons why your business e-mail is not secret.

2. Choose a password that is easy to remember while being a little obscure, using numbers, characters and symbols.

3. Consider encryption, which will scramble your messages so that only recipients with the key can decode them.

4. Do not give your private key to anyone — it's part of your electronic identity.

5. Consider sending personal messages as a file attachment and save it with a password.

6. Use a digital signature to confirm that your
   message was composed and signed by you
   and has not been tampered with.

7. Think twice before you hit the 'Send' button.

8. Treat all messages, even encrypted ones,
   as open documents that could end up on
   the screen of someone you don't like.

9. Never leave your desk while your mailer is online.

10. Install a good anti-virus program and keep it updated.

INDEX

ABOUT THE AUTHOR

Shirley Taylor has established herself as a leading authority in modern business writing and communication skills. She is the author of six successful books on communication skills, including the international bestseller, *Model Business Letters, E-mails and Other Business Documents*, which is now in its sixth edition, having sold almost half a million copies worldwide.

Shirley was born in the UK, and has lived and worked in Singapore, Bahrain and Canada. She has over 20 years of experience in teaching and training. After making Singapore her home in 2002, Shirley established her own company in 2007. ST Training Solutions Pte Ltd has quickly become highly regarded for providing a wide range of quality training programmes conducted by first-class trainers. The popularity of ST Training Solutions workshops, and the keen desire of participants to learn more, is what led to this 'Success Skills' series of books, which will prove an exciting supplement for those who are keen to develop their knowledge and skills.

Shirley conducts her own popular workshops on business writing and e-mail, as well as communication and secretarial skills. She puts a lot of passion and energy into her workshops to make sure they are entertaining, practical, informative and a lot of fun.

Having learnt a lot from her workshop participants over the years, Shirley has put much of her experience into the pages of this book. She's delighted that it will be one of the first to be published in ST Training Solutions 'Success Skills' series.

 **ST Training Solutions**

Success Skills Series

ST Training Solutions, based in Singapore, offers a wide range of popular, practical training programmes conducted by experienced, professional trainers. As CEO, Shirley Taylor takes a personal interest in working closely with trainers to ensure that each workshop is full of valuable tools, helpful guidelines and powerful action steps that will ensure a true learning experience for all participants. Some of the workshops offered are:

Power Up Your Business Writing Skills

Energise your E-mail Writing Skills

Success Skills for Secretaries and Support Staff

Successful Business Communication Skills

Creativity at Work

Present for Success

Speak up Successfully

Sharpen your Interpersonal Skills

Get to Grips with Grammar

Report Writing Essentials

Making Sense of Minutes

Writing to Unhappy Customers

Business Etiquette and Professional Poise

Emotional Intelligence at Work

Dealing with Difficult People and Situations

Achieving Peak Performance by Improving your Memory

Personal Effectiveness and You

Projecting a Professional Image

Shirley Taylor is also host of a very popular annual conference called ASSAP — the Asian Summit for Secretaries and Admin Professionals — organised in April each year by ST Training Solutions.

Find out more about ST Training Solutions at www.shirleytaylortraining.com.